DATE DUE

#47-0108 Peel Off Pressure Sensitive

GEORG SIMMEL
The Conflict in Modern Culture
and Other Essays

GEORG SIMMEL
The Conflict in Modern Culture
and Other Essays

Translated, with an introduction by

K. PETER ETZKORN

TEACHERS COLLEGE PRESS

Teachers College, Columbia University

New York

© 1968 BY TEACHERS COLLEGE PRESS
LIBRARY OF CONGRESS CATALOG CARD
NUMBER 67–25064

MANUFACTURED IN THE UNITED STATES OF AMERICA

This is Hildie's book.

Acknowledgements

The patience of those who assisted me in bringing this book into print cannot be adequately described; however, I wish to acknowledge how much I depended on the good will of others in preparing this set of translations. For orientation, encouragement, and numerous clarifications, my special appreciation goes to Theodore Abel, Carl Backman, Arturo Biblarz, Richard DeHaan, Leo Lowenthal, Benjamin Nelson, Alex Simirenko, Rudolph H. Weingartner, Kurt H. Wolff, and Dennis H. Wrong. I am grateful also to Arnold Simmel for permission to publish these translations of his grandfather's works and to the American Journal of Sociology for their translation of "A Chapter in the Philosophy of Value."

This undertaking would have been impossible indeed without the cooperation of staff at the University of California at Santa Barbara, the American University of Beirut, and the University of Nevada: the secretaries who typed and retyped the numerous revisions; Charles B. Spaulding and Samir Khalaf, who arranged facilities that permitted me to work on the translations; and, especially, Thomas O'Brien, Dean of the Graduate School at the University of Nevada, who made funds available for the final preparation of the manuscript.

K. PETER ETZKORN
Pensacola, Florida
March, 1968

Contents

Georg Simmel: An Introduction
   by K. Peter Etzkorn   1

1 The Conflict in Modern Culture   11

2 On the Concept and Tragedy of Culture   27

3 A Chapter in the Philosophy of Value   47

4 Sociological Aesthetics   68

5 On Aesthetic Quantities   81

6 On the Third Dimension in Art   86

7 The Dramatic Actor and Reality   91

8 Psychological and Ethnological Studies on Music   98

GEORG SIMMEL

The Conflict in Modern Culture
and Other Essays

Georg Simmel:
An Introduction

by K. Peter Etzkorn

O NE TEST OF THE IMPORTANCE of ideas and contributions of eminent men is undoubtedly whether they are considered relevant by future generations. Georg Simmel's work, although it was produced over fifty years ago, is still considered of major relevance to sociological and philosophical inquiry. It is partly in testimony to this that the present selection of several of his translated essays on cultural subjects is being made available.

Simmel (1858–1918) lived during a period of significant social and political change in Central Europe. The impact of technological developments made possible by the Industrial Revolution was increasingly changing the major modes of social life. Institutional structures were confronted with problems of adaptation. Frequent challenges were made to established modes of thought and novel ideas in response to social change. New and rapid modes of communication aided in the diffusion of ideas and made possible the emergence and sustenance of new forms of social life. To such topics much of Simmel's work is addressed and many of these topics have not lost their immediacy in spite of some substantive changes in technology and social life since then. We too are confronted with puzzles of urban growth, the "megalopolis," with technological change and political adaptation, and with the problem of the individual's integration into a largely impersonal society and the meaning of life, its values, and its cultivation and culture. Perhaps because of his having entered the discussion of these topics "earlier," before some of these issues became conventionally appropriated by emerging academic disciplines, he had the chance to develop an analytic attitude that in his hands promised to be highly productive. He could address himself to the issues of social life more directly than is possible within the restrictions of already established and frequently narrowly defined academic departments. Thus he fashioned his own sociological method for the study of social life in terms of what he conceived as the demands of the subject matter: the unending dialectic of human existence.

For Simmel, the continuity of the processes of life clashes necessarily with the acts of personal individuation, which are also the creative acts in which social institutions are established. These, in turn, gain a reality of their own which transcends their immediate *raison d'être*. Frequently in this process, what originally were considered as means come to be regarded as ends. In Simmel's dialectic, man is always in danger of being slain by those objects of his own creation which have lost their original human coefficient. This process, however, always occurs for Simmel within the framework of social relations regardless of specific historical periods. The dialectic is neither characteristic of capitalism, nor of socialism, nor of liberal democracy; it is much more. For Simmel, this dialectic between life and more-than-life represents the very nature of human existence, the very destiny of civilization, and thus it becomes the core of his scholarly inquiry.[1] In his sociological studies, Simmel addresses himself most directly to the study of the forms of human interaction. Human interaction, in this instance, represents another expression of the overriding dialectic of life, because man and fellow man are simultaneously dependent and independent of one another. When studying forms of interaction, Simmel is interested in the patterning of relationships between man and man—especially in those interaction dimensions that transcend any individual's attributes. As Friedrich H. Tenbruck has observed, by studying forms of interaction Simmel wishes to ascertain the extent to which the range of individual human conduct is restrained in keeping with the individual's cognizance of his diversified relationships with other individuals.[2] These persons, in turn, react and interact with him through concrete social relationships that at once restrain and stimulate him. These individuals, of course, are also constrained by his very own activities. Every individual who is in contact with another aids in the process of creating mutual expectations for what constitutes norms of appropriate conduct —modern sociologists would call this "normative role performance." Yet these emerging rules may soon grow so powerful in guiding any participant's choice of actions that they tend to rule him. The individual sees himself confronted with rules of his own making which have outgrown him. His initiative becomes juxtaposed to the requirements of his being part of a larger social whole. This basic dynamic of social life is explored by Simmel in its intriguing variations, whether they are manifested in man's relationships to phenomena of culture or to fellow man.

2

Georg Simmel, the youngest of seven children, was born in Berlin in 1858. In this capital he pursued all of his formal academic training, attending the gymnasium, completing university studies in history, philosophy, and Italian language and culture, obtaining his doctor's degree with a dissertation on Kant's *Physikalische Monadologie* (1881), and obtaining his first teaching position at the University of Berlin in 1885. He was to remain at this university until 1914, when, four years before his death, he was called to Strasbourg as full professor. He was highly respected by his students and enjoyed the satisfaction of frequently having to teach in the largest available lecture hall. That his style of delivery must have been extremely stimulating can be inferred from the many reminiscences of former students that are collected in Kurt Gassen's *Buch des Dankes an Georg Simmel.*[3] Over many years, he offered courses on history, social psychology, sociology, and on various subfields of philosophy, such as the philosophy of religion and of art.

Simmel's intense involvement in the different ways in which the drama of life unfolds is, perhaps, better suggested by glancing at his varied publications than at his university course offerings. In order to gain a full appreciation, one really needs to peruse the long bibliography of his works in Gassen's book. Some limited indication, however, is also represented in the following translations, which, related though they are by a common concern with culture, show Simmel applying different special emphases in its study. For further perspective, we also mention the translated titles of several of his major works: *Social Differentiation* (1890), *Problems of the Philosophy of History* (1892), *Introduction to the Philosophy of Morals* (1892–93), *The Philosophy of Money* (1900), *Sociology* (1908), *Goethe* (1913), *Rembrandt* (1916), *Major Problems of Philosophy* (1910), *The War and Spiritual Decisions* (1917), and *Perspectives on Life: Four Chapters in Metaphysics* (1918).

Whether he is dealing with the subjects of ethics and religion, with the biographies of creative men, or with the problems of artistic production, he seems always to be wrestling with the methodological implications of his basic dialectic position. He attempts to catch the subject in the net of his analytical dissection without thereby depriving it of its exciting quality, and he proceeds in this endeavor with great skill. Following him requires the close attention of the reader.

The selection of essays offered here in translation represents only a small fragment of Simmel's total work in this form. They are selected because of their topical concern with the question of man's relation to culture. In these essays, Simmel examines various implications the social life has for the status and development of culture in its impact on individuals and on social groups. He conceives of culture as the medium through which the basic dialectic of life is expressed. While it would be important to annotate some of the essays if they were to be regarded as definitive scientific statements, the primary goal was to make them available in English to the modern reader and to let Simmel speak as directly as possible through the medium of a translation. Nevertheless, a few introductory comments seem called for, to assist the modern reader in placing these essays in the context of the history of ideas.

Unfortunately, very little is known about the circumstances of their composition. As early as 1919, it was necessary for Köhler, in his sensitive appraisal of Simmel's work, to observe that it was not possible to learn from the essays when they were written, nor what influenced Simmel to write them, nor whether Simmel pursued any particular objective in furthering the cause of science or in attacking certain theoretical positions. Köhler wrote: "They are self-contained, as it were, timeless creations. They are enclosed by an invisible frame which guards their 'right of distance' in all directions." [4] These words were only too prophetic. A portion of Simmel's personal notes was lost in a train compartment after his death, and the major portion confiscated by the Nazi Gestapo in Hamburg harbor when Simmel's son, having been released from Dachau concentration camp, was allowed to emigrate with his family to the United States of America.[5]

The first essay, "The Conflict of Modern Culture," was a lecture not published until 1918, the last year of Simmel's life. It may well be one of his last statements concerning the broad issues of the dynamics of culture, aesthetics, and social life. We find Simmel analyzing the peculiar characteristics of the modern era in the revolt against the rule of forms in the realm of ideas, arts, and philosophy. He provides us with an explanation for the rise of these new phenomena, which later writers came to call Mass Culture. There are central themes reflecting social and cultural life in all epochs of human history, and it is these emerging themes in modern culture that need to be sought out, according to Simmel, if we wish to understand the movements in our own time.

In "The Concept and Tragedy of Culture," first published in 1911, Simmel develops the notion of the duality between the cultural meaning of objects, on the one hand, and their substantive meaning, on the other. This duality, however, always seems to demand a synthesis of subjective developments with the appropriate objectively spiritual values. Thus he views cultural phenomena as being in a precarious balance between having meaning by gaining social and individual recognition and merely existing without recognition and value for human life.

4

Through the use of numerous examples, Simmel helps the reader to approximate his position concerning the imperfect dimensions of this basic tragedy of culture, which to him reflects the general dialectic of life. In the process of becoming part of the culture, the individual is also being subjected to two independent and usually conflicting demands: the potentials of his human nature and the requirements of the social order.[6]

On the basis of this discussion, Simmel then turns to an analysis of some of the major problems of culture in modern life such as the problems of the fetishism of commodities, of alienation, and of a largely refined division of labor and bureaucracy.

In "A Chapter in the Philosophy of Value," published in 1900, Simmel explores the variety of social conditions under which social values are created and become attached to cultural objects. This essay is perhaps more direct in its approach than its philosophical title indicates. It offers a critical examination of a variety of explanations offered by previous writers on the subject of human values. Simmel proceeds to develop his own explanations of how objects come to attain valued positions in social behavior. Basic interpersonal relations, instead of quantitative measures, are presented as crucial elements in the process of value attribution. The exposition deals more with the economic than the cultural realm, but is equally applicable to both. An examination of particular social structures and their relationships to the valuation process concludes this essay.

The same topic is explored in the earlier essay, "Sociological Aesthetics," published in 1896. Here, the beauty value of objects is held not to reside in the objects themselves, but rather in the reciprocity between the individual beholder and the object. Depending on how deeply individuals involve themselves in social relationships that result in the social objectification of their individual preoccupations with the aesthetic stimulus of symmetry, the outcome will be of greater or less aesthetic value. This preoccupation is not necessarily restricted to what are traditionally considered areas of aesthetic concern. For Simmel even such developments as the politics of socialism or certain forms of social organization such as bureaucracy are partially explained by an aesthetic drive towards symmetry. It appears that certain forms of social organization and works of art seem to attain value for the same reasons; they may represent or express objective dimensions of the same subjective desires.

This point is further explored in Simmel's talk in 1903 to a gathering of psychologists, "Concerning Aesthetic Quantities." He argues that even such physiological sensations as those, for example, that result from varying the spatial dimensions of representations in painting, are perceived and mentally interpreted according to expectations identical with those that govern interpersonal relationships: "Man (as a *social* being) is the measure of all things also with respect to visual perspective."

In a later essay, "On the Third Dimension in Art" (1906), aesthetic problems of painting and their societal manifestations become the focus of Simmel's analysis. He argues that our perceptions are influenced by the categories under which we organize sense impressions. An analysis of the social conventions relating to the perception of a third dimension in painting serves as the starting point for a discussion which then leads to a consideration of the artistic meaning of tactile values and to an excursion into general aesthetics.

Similarly in "The Dramatic Actor and Reality" (1912), Simmel addresses himself to the special aesthetic questions of the legitimate theater and to the social implications of one person playing the role of another. The conditions under which a play is "more than life"— that is, art—are worked out. The artistic actor is the creator of a new world and not the imitator of an old reality. Thus, to Simmel dramatic art is genuinely rooted both in the aesthetic unity of the poetic work and in the social realities of the playwright, actor, and audience.

In closing the present selection of translations with Simmel's first published essay, "Psychological and Ethnological Studies on Music," we cannot help noting the fact that, from his earliest publications on, his work consistently revolved around the question of the place of the individual in the realm of culture. This is so even though this early study is more under the influence of the academic conventions of the late nineteenth century—such as the interest in evolutionary thought— than are his later, perhaps more personal, essays. In this lengthy study, Simmel questions a variety of evolutionary hypotheses concerning the origin of music as an art form in human society. He does this by mentally "testing" these propositions in the light of ethnographic evidence concerning musical practice in a variety of cultures. Then he proceeds with his own explanations, which establish music as a communication medium of highly diffuse information. In examining the implications of this position, he explores the dialectic relationship between the cultural product of music and the society and conditions under which music becomes meaningful. Musical values, just like other artistic and general aesthetic or simply human values can best be understood if viewed in interdependence with the specific social groups formed or somehow affected by them and affecting them in turn. Here, as in his later writing, it is the interdependence between the social actors and the results of the interactions that holds his fascination and comes to form the central subject of his inquiry.

If one considers Simmel's basic concerns and their obvious relationship to the body of traditional subjects of the various contemporary social sciences, one may wonder why more of his extensive work has not yet been made available in English translation to facilitate access to his ideas. The present essays, for instance, illustrate how Simmel, in his perceptive analysis of "The Dramatic Actor and Reality," antecedes Ralph Linton's discussion of role and status by many years. Only Lewis A. Coser, to my knowledge, has pointed this out, in an aside in his introduction to a collection of essays evaluating Simmel's sociological contributions.[7] "The Dramatic Actor and Reality" also contains notions on role distance that remind us of Erving Goffman's later studies in the sociology of interaction.[8] To give another example, a number of ideas in Simmel's "Sociological Aesthetics" throw light on the long standing debate within sociology between sociological nominalists and realists. To this day, however, the solution offered by Simmel, as outlined in his essay "On the Conflict and Tragedy of Culture" and in his other more specifically sociological writings, has not been accepted universally. There are still scholars who view society as the composite of many individuals or others who view it as some super-organism. Simmel suggested that the more appropriate conception is to view all life as being structured in various forms of mutual interaction among individuals who are structured in various relationships.

There may be many reasons why Simmel's impact has been relatively limited, even in Germany. In Germany, for example, he is perhaps more nearly identified as a philosopher, while in the United States, he belongs among the "fathers" of sociology. It would seem that in either country his influence has come not from the recognition of the total conception of his work, but only from the recognition of some selected aspect of it.[9] We may speculate on the reasons for this partial appreciation and recognition, either of which fails to do justice to him, if only because for him the analysis of social life could not truly be compartmentalized.

The limited appeal of Simmel's work may have been related to his consistent insistence on social interaction (*Wechselwirkung*), on the mutual interdependence between culture and individual, and between individual and fellow man. Concerning his method, Raymond Aron observes that Simmel's approach has found many admirers but few disciples.[10] There can be no doubt that becoming a disciple of Simmel's would demand a great deal of dedication, often only because of the difficulty and complexity of his arguments. A more significant reason, I believe, has been offered by Nicholas Spykman, who also can be credited with having provided the first major presentation of Simmel's epistemology in the United States. He points out that Simmel's perspective on substantive topics is always couched as a function of several variables rather than as a function of one. Since the latter, more traditional, mode of conceptualizing scientific problems had been accepted during Simmel's lifetime and had been demonstrated, more so than his own approach, to produce pragmatic results, his mode of approach was probably extremely difficult to translate into systematic methods for the study of scientific topics. Moreover, this difficulty was probably increased by the fact that he himself did not offer systematic expositions of the methodological implications of his position for the study of social dynamics.[11]

Beginning during the latter part of Simmel's life, but primarily since his death, scientific models for the study of social phenomena that relate several variables simultaneously to one another have gained some acceptance. Perhaps Simmel was too advanced in scientific vision for his own age and may now be more easily understood in the intellectual climate of the present. There is some indication that this is so. The 1950's brought a number of new translations of Simmel's work in sociology as well as the reprinting of earlier translations in anthologies.[12] On the centennial of his birthday (1958), commemorative volumes were prepared in German and English, with the English volume providing additional translations.[13] Attention to Simmel's work continued in the 1960's with Rudolph H. Weingartner's study and Lewis A. Coser's book of essays.[14] Frequent reference to Simmel's work in contemporary studies of small-group dynamics and of certain other work in social psychology suggests his usefulness to students of these subjects. Perhaps this collection of translations may stimulate interest in exploring Simmel's ideas in the area of culture, an area which will assume even greater significance as modern societies come to provide means which allow man to turn more of his attention to culture and away from the pursuit of the sheer necessities of life.

A Note on the Translations

In translating Simmel one is faced with the problem of how to render in English a variety of terms central to Simmel's conception of human life. On the whole, Simmel's terminology is similar to that so characteristic of his contemporary Dilthey, in his *Geisteswissenschaften*. The problem of translating the German of this period has already been discussed by Gerth and Mills, Kurt H. Wolff, and H. P. Rickmann.[15] In general, we have followed their example for the sake of helping gradually to establish a conventionalized English rendition. In addition, we have adopted Rudolph H. Weingartner's practice of rendering the German *Seele* as "psyche" wherever this seemed appropriate.[16] In several instances "self" represented the best English equivalent. All essays but "A Chapter in the Philosophy of Value" are translated by the editor.

Notes to Introduction

1. For a fuller discussion of Simmel's dialectic of social life, see particularly Albert Saloman, "German Sociology," Chapter 20 in Georges Gurvitch and Wilbert E. Moore, eds., *20th Century Sociology* (New York: Philosophical Library, 1945).

2. Friedrich H. Tenbruck, "Georg Simmel," *Kölner Zeitschrift für Soziologie und Sozialpsychologie*, 10 (1958), 587–614, p. 598.

3. Kurt Gassen and Michael Landmann, eds., *Buch des Dankes an Georg Simmel: Briefe, Erinnerungen, Bibliographie* (Berlin: Duncker and Humblot, 1958).

4. Max Frischeisen-Köhler, "Georg Simmel," *Kantstudien*, 24 (1919), 1–51, p. 5.

5. Gassen and Landmann, *op. cit.*, p. 14.

6. Rudolph H. Weingartner, *Experience and Culture: The Philosophy of Georg Simmel* (Middletown, Connecticut: Wesleyan University Press, 1962), explores the peculiar meaning of Simmel's culture concept in his discussion of *Lebensphilosophie*, p. 71 *passim*.

7. Lewis A. Coser, ed., *Georg Simmel* (Englewood Cliffs, New Jersey: Prentice-Hall, Inc., 1965), p. 5.

8. Erving Goffman, *Encounters* (Indianapolis, Indiana: Bobbs-Merrill, 1961).

9. For an appraisal of the impact of Simmel's work on different schools of sociology and philosophy see also Tenbruck, *op. cit.*

10. Raymond Aron, *German Sociology* (London: William Heinemann, Ltd., 1957), p. 6.

11. Nicholas J. Spykman, *The Social Theory of Georg Simmel* (Chicago: University of Chicago Press, 1925), p. 6.

12. Kurt H. Wolff, tr., ed., *The Sociology of Georg Simmel* (Glencoe: The Free Press, 1950). Kurt H. Wolff and Reinhard Bendix, trs. Georg Simmel, *Conflict and the Web of Group-Affliations* (Glencoe: The Free Press, 1955). Edgar F. Borgatta and Henry J. Meyer, eds., *Sociological Theory: Present Day Sociology from the Past* (New York: Alfred A. Knopf, 1956). Lewis A. Coser and Bernhard Rosenberg, eds., *Sociological Theory: A Book of Readings* (New York: The Macmillan Co., 1957).

13. Gassen and Landmann, *op. cit.* Kurt H. Wolff, ed., *Georg Simmel, 1858–1918* (Columbus, Ohio: The Ohio State University Press, 1959).

14. Weingartner, *op. cit.*, and Coser, *op. cit.*

15. See H. H. Gerth and C. Wright Mills, trs., eds., preface to *From Max Weber: Essays in Sociology* (New York: Oxford University Press, 1946). Kurt H. Wolff, tr., ed., "A Note on the Translation," in *The Sociology* (*op. cit.*) pp. lxiii–lxiv. Wilhelm Dilthey, *Pattern and Meaning in History,* ed. and introduced by H. P. Rickmann (New York: Harper Torchbooks, 1961), pp. 22–24.

16. Weingartner, *op. cit.*

1

*The Conflict in Modern Culture**

W HENEVER LIFE PROGRESSES beyond the animal level to that of spirit, and spirit progresses to the level of culture, an internal contradiction appears. The whole history of culture is the working out of this contradiction. We speak of culture whenever life produces certain forms in which it expresses and realizes itself: works of art, religions, sciences, technologies, laws, and innumerable others. These forms encompass the flow of life and provide it with content and form, freedom and order. But although these forms arise out of the life process, because of their unique constellation they do not share the restless rhythm of life, its ascent and descent, its constant renewal, its incessant divisions and reunifications. These forms are frameworks for the creative life which, however, soon transcends them. They should also house the imitative life, for which, in the final analysis, there is no space left. They acquire fixed identities, a logic and lawfulness of their own; this new rigidity inevitably places them at a distance from the spiritual dynamic which created them and which makes them independent.

Herein lies the ultimate reason why culture has a history. Insofar as life, having become spirit, ceaselessly creates such forms which become self-enclosed and demand permanence, these forms are inseparable from life; without them it cannot be itself. Left to itself, however, life streams on without interruption; its restless rhythm opposes the fixed duration of any particular form. Each cultural form, once it is created, is gnawed at varying rates by the forces of life. As soon as one is fully developed, the next begins to form; after a struggle that may be long or short, it will inevitably succeed its predecessor.

History, as an empirical science, concerns itself with changes in the

* A translation of *Der Konflict der modernen Kultur,* 2nd ed. (Munich: Duncker and Humblot, 1921), 30 pp.

forms of culture, and aims to discover the real carriers and causes of change in each particular case. But we can also discern a deeper process at work. Life, as we have said, can manifest itself only in particular forms; yet, owing to its essential restlessness, life constantly struggles against its own products, which have become fixed and do not move along with it. This process manifests itself as the displacement of an old form by a new one. This constant change in the content of culture, even of whole cultural styles, is the sign of the infinite fruitfulness of life. At the same time, it marks the deep contradiction between life's eternal flux and the objective validity and authenticity of the forms through which it proceeds. It moves constantly between death and resurrection—between resurrection and death.

This characteristic of cultural processes was first noted in economic change. The economic forces of every epoch develop forms of production which are appropriate to their nature. Slave economics, guild constitutions, agrarian modes of soil labor—all these, when they were formed, expressed adequately the wishes and capacities of their times. Within their own norms and boundaries, however, there grew economic forces whose extension and development these systems obstructed. In time, through gradual explosive revolutions, they burst the oppressive bonds of their respective forms and replaced them with modes of production more appropriate. A new mode of production, however, need not have overwhelming energy of its own. Life itself, in its economic dimension—with its drive and its desire for advancement, its internal changes and differentiation—provides the dynamics for this whole movement. Life as such is formless, yet incessantly generates forms for itself. As soon as each form appears, however, it demands a validity which transcends the moment and is emancipated from the pulse of life. For this reason, life is always in a latent opposition to the form. This tension soon expresses itself in this sphere and in that; eventually it develops into a comprehensive cultural necessity. Thus life perceives "the form as such" as something which has been forced upon it. It would like to puncture not only this or that form, but form *as such*, and to absorb the form in its immediacy, to let its own power and fullness stream forth just as if it emanated from life's own source, until all cognition, values, and forms are reduced to direct manifestations of life.

At present, we are experiencing a new phase of the old struggle—no longer a struggle of a contemporary form, filled with life, against an old, lifeless one, but a struggle of life against the form *as such*, against the *principle* of form. Moralists, reactionaries, and people with strict feelings for style are perfectly correct when they complain about the increasing "lack of form" in modern life. They fail to understand, however, that what is happening is not only a negative, passive dying out of traditional forms, but simultaneously a fully positive drive towards life which is actively repressing these forms. Since this struggle, in extent and intensity, does not permit concentration on the creation of new forms, it makes a virtue of necessity and insists on a fight against forms simply because they are forms. This is probably only possible in an epoch where cultural forms are conceived of as an exhausted soil which has yielded all that it could grow, which, however, is still completely covered by products of its former fertility.

Similar events certainly took place during the eighteenth century. Then, however, they occurred over a longer period, from the English Enlightenment of the seventeenth century to the French Revolution. Moreover, there was an almost completely new ideal standing behind these revolutions: the liberation of the individual, the application of reason to life, the progress of mankind towards happiness and perfection. New cultural forms developed easily in this milieu—almost as if they had somehow been prepared—and provided inner security to mankind. The conflict of the new forms against the old did not generate the cultural pressure we know today, when life in all possible manifestations agitates against being directed into any fixed forms whatever.

The concepts of *life*, which several decades ago became dominant in the philosophical interpretation of the world, prepared the way for our situation. In order to place this phenomenon within the arena of the history of ideas, I will have to range a little further afield. In every important cultural epoch, one can perceive a central idea from which spiritual movements originate and towards which they seem to be oriented. Each central idea is modified, obscured and opposed in innumerable ways. Nevertheless, it represents the "secret being" of the epoch. In every single epoch, the central idea resides wherever the most perfect being, the most absolute and metaphysical phase of reality join with the highest values, with the most absolute demands on ourselves and on the world. Certainly, there follow logical contradictions. Whatever is unconditionally real does not require to be realized, nor can one evidently say that an existing most unquestioned being is only supposed to come into being. *Weltanschauungen* in their ultimate perfections do not concern themselves with such conceptual difficulties. Wherever they commit one, where otherwise opposing series of existence and ethical obligation are joined, one can be assured to locate a really central idea of the respective world view.

I will indicate with greatest brevity a few of these central ideas. For Greek classicism, it was the idea of *being*, of the uniform, the substantial, the divine. This divinity was not presented pantheistically without form, but was molded into meaningfully plastic forms. The Christian

Middle Ages placed in its stead the concept of *God* as at once the source and goal of all reality, unquestioned lord over our existence and yet demanding free obedience and devotion from us. Since the Renaissance, this place has come to be occupied gradually by the concept of *nature*. It appeared as the only being and truth, yet also as an ideal, as something which first had to be represented and insisted upon. At first this occurred among artists, for whom the final kernel of reality embodied the highest value. The seventeenth century built its ideas around the concept of *natural law*, which alone it saw as essentially valid. The century of Rousseau enshrined *nature* as its ideal, its absolute value, the goal of its longing. Toward the end of this epoch, *ego*, the spiritual personality, emerged as a new central concept. Some thinkers represented the totality of being as a creation of the ego; others saw personal identity as a *task*, the essential task for man. Thus the ego, human individuality, appeared either as an absolute moral demand or as the metaphysical purpose of the world. Despite the colorful variety of its intellectual movements, the nineteenth century did not develop a comprehensive central idea—unless, perhaps, we give this title to the idea of *society*, which for many nineteenth-century thinkers epitomized the reality of life. Thus the individual was often seen as a mere point of intersection for social series, or even as a fiction like the atom. Alternately, complete submergence of the self in society was demanded; to devote oneself completely to society was viewed as an absolute obligation, which included morality and everything else. Only at the very end of the century did a new idea appear: the concept of *life* was raised to a central place, in which perceptions of reality were united with metaphysical, psychological, moral, and aesthetic values.

The expansion and development of the concept of life is confirmed by the fact that it brought together two important philosophical antagonists, Schopenhauer and Nietzsche. Schopenhauer is the first modern philosopher who does not inquire for some *contents* of life, for ideas or states of being (*Seinsbeständen*) within the deepest and most decisive strata. Instead, he asks exclusively: What is life, what is its meaning, purely *as* life? One must not be misled by the fact that he does not use the term "life," but speaks only about the *will* towards life of the will itself. The will represents his answer concerning the question about the meaning of life which transcends all his speculative extrapolations beyond life. This means that life cannot obtain any meaning and purpose from beyond itself. It will always grasp its own will though it be disguised in a thousand forms. Since it can only remain within itself, because of its metaphysical reality, it can find only unbounded illusion and ultimate disappointment in each apparent goal. Nietzsche, on the other hand, who also starts from life as the singular determination of itself and the sole substance of all its contents, finds in life itself the purpose of life which it is denied from the outside. This life by its nature is increment, enrichment, development towards fulfillment and power, towards a force and beauty flowing from itself. It gains greater value not through reaching a designated goal, but through its own development by becoming *more* alive and thus gaining a value which increases towards the infinite. Although Schopenhauer's desperation about life is radically opposed to Nietzsche's jubilation because of deep, essential contrasts which deride any intellectual mediation or decision, these two thinkers share a basic question which separates them from all earlier philosophers. This basic question is: What is the meaning of life, what is its value merely as life? One can only inquire into knowledge and morality, self and reason, art and God, happiness and suffering, once this first puzzle has been solved. Its solution decides everything else. It is only the original fact of life which provides meaning and measure, positive or negative value. The concept of life is the point of intersection for these two opposed lines of thought which provide the framework for the fundamental decisions of modern life.

I will now illustrate through several contemporary examples the uniqueness of the cultural situation we are (in 1914) undergoing, in which the longing for a new form always overturns the old one, in particular, the opposition against the principle of form as such. We find this opposition even when consciousness appears to progress towards new structures. The Middle Ages had their ecclesiastical Christian ideals, and the Renaissance had its rediscovery of secular nature. The Enlightenment embraced the ideal of reason, and German idealism embellished science by artistic fantasies and provided for art a foundation of cosmic width through scientific knowledge. But the basic impulse behind contemporary culture is a negative one, and this is why, unlike men in all these earlier epochs, we have been for some time now living without any shared ideal, even perhaps without any ideals at all.

If you were to ask educated people today by what ideals they live, most would give a specialized answer derived from their occupational experience. Only rarely would they speak of a cultural ideal which rules them as total human beings. There is a good reason for this. Not only is there a lack of material for a comprehensive cultural ideal, but the fields which it would have to circumscribe are too numerous and heterogeneous to permit such intellectual simplification. Moving to individual cases, I will address myself first to art.

Of the various endeavors which collectively are designated as *Futurism*, only the movement which calls itself *Expressionism* seems to have a sharply delineated identity of its own. If I am not mistaken, the meaning of Expressionism is that the inner emotions of the artist are manifest in his work exactly as he experiences them; his emotions are continued, extended in the work. Human emotions cannot be reified in artistic convention, or moulded by a form which is forced on them from without. For this reason Expressionism has nothing in common with that imitation of a being or of an event which is the intention of Impressionism. Impressions, after all, are not purely individual products of the artist, exclusively determined from within, but passive and dependent on a world outside. The work of art which reflects them is a sort of mixture between the artistic life and the peculiarity of a given object. Any artistic form must reach the artist from somewhere: from tradition, from a previous example, from a fixed principle. But all these sources of form are restraints on life, which wishes to flow creatively from within itself. If life yields to such forms, it only finds itself bent, rigidified, and distorted in the work of art.

Let us consider, in its purest form, the expressionistic model of the creative process. The movements of the painter's spirit, according to this model, extend without any interference to the hand which holds the brush. The painting expresses them, just as a gesture expresses inner emotions or a shout expresses pain: the movements of the brush follow those of the spirit without resistance; hence the image on the canvas represents an immediate condensation of inner life, which did not permit anything superficial or alien to enter into its unfolding. Expressionistic paintings have often been named after some object with which they seem to have nothing in common, and many people consider this strange and irrational. In fact, however, it is not as meaningless as it would appear according to previous artistic preconceptions. The inner emotions of the artist, which flow forth in an expressionistic work, may originate in secret or unknown sources within the soul. But they can also originate in stimuli from objects in the external world. Until recently it was assumed that a successful artistic response must be morphologically similar to the stimulus that evoked it; indeed the whole impressionistic school was based on this conception. It was one of the great achievements of Expressionism to dispel this idea. Instead it demonstrated that there is no need for the identity between the form of the cause and that of its effect. Thus, the perception of a violin or a human face can evoke in a painter emotional responses which his art metamorphoses into a completely different form. One might say that the expressionistic artist replaces his model with the impulse lying behind the model that stimulates his life, which obeys only itself, towards movement. Expressed in an abstract manner, which nevertheless traces the realistic line of the wall, the creative act represents the struggle of

16

life for self-identity. Whenever life expresses itself, it desires to express only itself; thus it breaks through any form which would be superimposed on it by some other reality.

The established phenomenon, the painting, does of course have a form. But according to the artist's intention, the form represents only a necessary evil. Unlike all previous artistic forms, it does not have a meaning by itself. For this reason, abstract art is also indifferent to the traditional standards of beauty or ugliness, which are connected with the primacy of form. Life, in its flow, is not determined by a goal but driven by a force: hence it has its significance beyond beauty and ugliness. Once the product exists, it becomes evident that it does not possess the kind of meaning and value which one expects from an objectified datum that has become independent of its creator. This value, however, has been withheld from the painting—we might say, almost jealously —by a life which gives expression only to itself. Our peculiar preference for the late works of major artists may be based on this fact. Creative life has here become so sovereign in these works, so self-sufficient and rich, that it rejects any other form which is traditional or shared with others. Its expression in a work of art is nothing but its natural fate. As connected and meaningful as the work may appear from this perspective, it may appear fragmented, unbalanced, as if composed of pieces, when viewed from the point of view of traditional forms. This is not an example of a senile incapacity for making a form, no weakness of age, but rather strength of age. In this epoch of his perfection, the great artist is so pure that his work will reveal through its form what has been autonomously generated through the drive of his life. The unique right of the form has been lost to the artist.

In principle it is completely possible that a form which is perfect and meaningful purely as a form will represent a fully adequate expression of immediate life, clinging to it as if it were an organically grown skin. This is undoubtedly so in the case of the great classical works of art. Disregarding them, however, we find a peculiar property of the spiritual realm which has implications far beyond its consequences for the arts. We might say that the arts express something which is alive beyond the scope of perfected and available artistic forms. Every major artist and each great work of art contain more breadth and depth which flow from hidden sources than art is able to express. Men try incessantly to shape and interpret this life. In classical examples the attempt is successful, and life fuses completely with art. However, life attains a more highly differentiated and more self-conscious expression in those cases where it contradicts and even destroys artistic forms. There is, for example, the inner fate which Beethoven intends to express in his last compositions. The old artistic form is not broken up; rather, it is overpowered by something else, something which breaks forth from another dimension.

It is similar in the case of metaphysics. Its goal is the search of truth; yet something more is often expressed through it. This something becomes unrecognizable, since it overpowers the truth as such, since what it asserts is full of contradictions and can be easily disproven. It can be counted among the typical paradoxes of the spirit—that only some systems of metaphysics would be given the status of truth if they were measured by the standard of actual experience. Perhaps, similarly, there is also some element in religion which is not religious; when this element comes to the surface, all concretized religious forms, in which there is true religion, may be destroyed. This is the inner dynamic of heresy and apostasy.

There is more in human products, perhaps in every single one which derives fully from the creative power of the spirit, than is contained in its forms. This marks off everything that has soul from all that is produced merely mechanically. Here, perhaps, may be found the motivation for the contemporary interest in the art of Van Gogh. In him more than any other painter, one senses a passionate life which swings far beyond the limits of pictorial art. It flows from a unique breadth and depth; that it finds in the painter's talent a channel for its expression seems only accidental, as if it could just as well have given life to practical or religious, to poetic or musical activities. It is primarily this burning life, which can be felt in its immediacy—and which sometimes enters into a destructive contrast with its obvious form—that makes Van Gogh so fascinating.

The desire for completely abstract art among some sectors of modern youth may stem from passion for an immediate and unrestrained (*nackten*) expression of self. The frenetic pace of the lives of our youth carries this tendency to its absolute extreme, and it is youth above all which represents this movement. In general, historical changes of an internal or external revolutionary impact have been carried by youth. In the special nature of the present change, we have a particular reference to it. Whereas adults because of their weakening vitality, concentrate their attention more and more on the objective *contents* of life, which in the present meaning could as well be designated as its forms, youth is more concerned with the process of life. Youth only wishes to express its power and its surplus of power, regardless of the objects involved. Thus cultural movement toward life and its expression alone, which disdains almost everything formal, objectifies the meaning of youthful life.

A fundamental observation must be made here which also applies outside the art world. What are we to make of the widespread *search for originality* among contemporary youth? Often it is only a form of vanity, the attempt to become a "sensation" both for oneself and others. The motive in better cases is a passion for giving expression to the truly individual life. The certainty that life is really only its expression seems to take hold of youth only in times such as ours, when nothing traditional is accepted. To accept any objective form, it is felt, would drain away human individuality: moreover it would dilute one's vitality by freezing it into the mold of something already dead. Originality reassures us that life is pure, that it has not diluted itself by absorbing extrinsic, objectified, rigid forms into its flow. This is perhaps a subliminal motive, not explicit but powerful, which underlies modern individualism.

We can find this same basic desire in one of the most recent philosophical movements which turns its back most decisively against traditional expressions of philosophy. I will designate it as *Pragmatism*, since the best known branch of this theory, the American, has thus been named. I consider this particular branch as most superficial and limited. We can construct an ideal type of Pragmatism independent of any existing fixed version, which will illuminate its relation to our present inquiry. Let us first understand what Pragmatism is attacking. Of all areas of culture, there is none which we consider more independent of life, none so autonomous in its isolation from the motives, needs, and fates of individuals than cognition. That two times two equals four, or that material masses are attracted to one another inversely to the square of their distances, is valid whether or not living minds know it, regardless of any changes of mind which mankind might undergo. Even technical knowledge, which is directly interwoven with life and plays a large role in the history of mankind, remains essentially untouched by the ups and downs of life's flow. So-called "practical" knowledge, after all, is only "theoretical" knowledge which has been applied to practical purposes. As a form of knowledge it belongs to an order with laws of its own, an idealized empire of truth.

It is this independence of truth, which has been presupposed throughout history, that Pragmatism most avidly denies. Our external life no less than our internal life, the pragmatist claims, is based on some imagination of knowledge. If it is true it will preserve and support our life; if it is an error, it will lead us into ruin. Our imaginations are formed by purely psychic influences. In no way are they mechanical reflections of the reality in which our real lives are intertwined. Hence it would be a most remarkable coincidence if they were to lead to desirable and predictable consequences within the realm of the real. It is probable, however, that among the numerous impressions and ideas which determine our active life, there are those which obtain the title of truth because they support and sustain life, while others with opposing consequences are called erroneous. Hence there is no originally independent truth which is subsequently drawn into the stream of life in order to guide it appropriately. On the contrary, among the infinite number of images and ideas which are borne along on the stream of our consciousness, there are some which correspond with our will to live. One might say that this is an accident; without this accident, however, we could not exist. It is precisely these supportive ideas which we recognize as right and true. Thus it is neither the objects by themselves, nor sovereign reason, which determine the truth-value of our thoughts. Rather, it is life—which expresses itself sometimes through the stark necessities of survival, sometimes through the deepest spiritual needs—that forces us to classify our ideas, one pole of which we designate as the full truth and the other as full error.

I cannot give a full exposition of this theory or criticize it here. Nor am I here concerned with its truth or falsity. I want simply to observe that it has been developed at a particular stage in history. Pragmatism, as we have seen, deprives truth (*Erkennen*) of its old claim to be a free-floating domain ruled by independent and ideal laws. Truth has now become interwoven with life, nourished by this source, guided by the totality of its directions and purposes, legitimized through its basic values. Life has thus reclaimed its sovereignty over a previously antonomous province. This can be reformulated in a more ideological way: The form of truth (*Erkennen*) in the past provided a fixed frame or an indestructible canvas for the total world of our thoughts and feelings, which it claimed to infuse with an inner consistency and a self-sufficient meaning. Now, however, thought and feeling are being dissolved in and by the stream of life; they yield to its growing and changing forces and directions, without providing them with any resistance based on an independent right or a timeless validity. The purest expression of Life as a central idea is reached when it is viewed as the metaphysical basic fact, as the essence of all being. This goes far beyond the transformation of the problem of knowledge: now every object becomes a pulse beat of absolute life, or one manner of its presentation, or a developmental stage. In the total unfolding of the world toward the spirit, life rises as spirit. As matter, it sinks below. When this theory resolves the problem of knowledge through an intuition which, beyond all logic and rational intelligibility, immediately grasps the intrinsic truth of things, it means to say that only life is capable of understanding life. From this perspective all objectivity, the object of all knowledge, must be transformed into life. Thus the process of cognition, now interpreted as a function of life is confronted with an object which it can completely penetrate since it is equal in its essence. While original pragmatism revolved the image of the world into life from the point of view of the subject only, it (*Lebensphiloso-phie*) did this for the object as well. Nothing is retained here of form as a principle independent of life, as a mode of being with meaning and power of its own. What might still be designated form, when staying within the terms of this imagery, could only exist because of reprieve given by this life.

This movement away from formal principles reaches a zenith not only in the pragmatists, but in all thinkers who are filled with the modern feeling against closed systems. Earlier epochs, ruled by classical and formal considerations, had raised these systems to a level of sanctity. The closed system aims to unite all truths, in their most general concepts, into a structure of higher and lower elements which extend from a basic theme, arranged symmetrically and balanced in all directions. The decisive point is that it sees the proof of its sub-stantive validity in its architectural and aesthetic completion, in the successful closure and solidity of its edifice. This represents the most extreme culmination of the formal principle: perfection of form as the ultimate criterion of truth. This is the view against which life, which is continuously creating and destroying forms, must defend itself.

The philosophy that exalts and glorifies life insists firmly on two things. On one hand it rejects mechanics as a universal principle: it views mechanics as, at best, a technique in life, more likely a sympton of its decay. On the other hand it rejects the claim of ideas to a meta-physical independence and primacy. Life does not wish to be domi-nated by what is below it; indeed, it does not wish to be dominated at all, not even by ideas which claim for themselves a rank above it. Although no higher form of life is capable of knowing itself without the guidance of ideas this now seems to be possible only because ideas themselves derive from life. It is the essence of life to generate its guidance, salvation, opposition, victories, and victims. It sustains and elevates itself, as it were, by an indirect route, through products of its own. That they confront it independently represents its own achieve-ment, expresses its own distinctive style of life. This internal opposition is the tragic conflict of life as spirit. It gets more noticeable the more self-conscious life becomes.

Viewed in the most general cultural perspective, this movement implies a turn away from classicism as the absolute ideal for human culture. Classicism, after all, is the ideology of form, which regards itself as the ultimate norm for life and creation. Certainly nothing more adequate or refined has taken the place of the old ideal. The attack against classicism is not concerned with the introduction of new cultural forms. Instead self-assured life wishes to liberate itself from the yoke of form as such, of which classicism is a historical representation.

I can report briefly on an identical trend within a specialized area of ethics. A systematic critique of existing sexual relationships has been named "the new morality." It is propagated by a small group, but its aims are shared by a large one. Its criticism is directed mainly against two elements of the contemporary scene: marriage and prostitution. Its basic theme can be expressed as follows: the most personal and intimate meaning of erotic life is destroyed by the forms in which our culture has reified and trapped it. Marriage, which is entered for a thousand nonerotic reasons, is destroyed from within by a thousand unyielding traditions and legalized cruelties; where it is not wrecked, it loses all individuality and leads to stagnation. Prostitution has almost turned into a legal institution which forces the erotic life of young people into a dishonorable direction which contradicts and caricatures its innermost nature. Marriage and prostitution alike appear as oppressive forms which thwart immediate and genuine life. Under different cultural circumstances, these forms may not have been so inappropriate. Now, however, they call forth forces of opposition which sprung from the ultimate sources of life. We can see here how large a shadow falls between the will to destroy old forms and the desire to build new ones. These reformers are not really interested in working out an adequate replacement for the forms which they condemn. The destructive force of their criticism impedes the cultural process of obsolescence and reconstruction which would normally take place. The force acting in the guise of new forms, is temporarily and as it were without disguise directed against those old forms emptied of genuine erotic life. Now, however, it is confronted with the previously mentioned contradiction since erotic life, as soon as it is expressed in cultural contexts, necessarily requires some form. Nevertheless, it is only a superficial observer who sees here nothing but unbounded and anarchic lust. Genuine erotic life in fact flows naturally in individual channels. Opposition is directed against forms because they force it into generalized schemata and thereby overpower its uniqueness. The struggle between life and form is fought here less abstractly and less metaphysically as a struggle between individuality and generalization.

We can find the same tendency in contemporary religion. Observe, for instance, the fact that quite a few intellectually advanced individuals employ mysticism to satisfy their religious needs. This has been noticed since around the turn of the century. On the whole it can be assumed that these people were socialized into the ideologies of one or another of the existing churches. A double motivation for their mysticism is unmistakable. First of all, the forms which objectify and direct religious feeling are felt to be inadequate for contemporary life. On the other hand, these mystical tendencies suggest that life's longing may be frustrated by objective forms in themselves, that the religious impulse must search for different goals and ways. It seems clear that a firm determination and delimitation of the boundaries of religious experience has been replaced. Mysticism aspires toward a deity which transcends every personal and particular form; it seeks an undetermined expanse of religious feeling which does not conflict with any dogmatic barrier, a deepening into formless infinity, a mode of expression based only on the powerful longing of the soul. Mysticism appears as the last refuge for religious individuals who cannot as yet free themselves from all transcendental guidance, but only, as it were preliminarily, from that which is determined and fixed in content.

The most decisive instance of this development—even though it may be full of contradictions and be eternally separated from its objective—is a tendency for forms of religious *belief* to dissolve into modes of religious *life*, into religiosity as a purely *functional* justification of religion. Until recently, changes of religious culture have always proceeded in the following way: a certain form of religious life, originally fully adequate in its strengths and essential characteristics, gradually rigidifies in superficialties and narrow specialization. It is displaced by a newly rising form in which religious impulses can flow, dynamically and without impediment. In other words, a new religious form, a new series of beliefs took the place of an outmoded one. For a relatively large number of people today, the supernatural objects of religious belief have been radically excised; their religious impulse, however, has not thereby been eliminated. Its effective force, which formerly manifested itself through the development of more adequate dogmatic contents, can no longer express itself through the polarity of a believing subject and a believed object. In the ultimate state of affairs towards which this new tendency is aiming, religion would function as a medium for the direct expression of life. It would be analogous not to a single melody within the symphony of life, but to the tonality within which the whole work is performed. The space of life, filled entirely by secular contents, actions and fate, thoughts and feelings, would be permeated with that unique inner unity between humility and authority, tension and peace, danger and consecration, which can only be called religious. Life spent in this fashion would demonstrate its absolute value—a value which, under other circumstances, was given to it only through the singular forms in which it appeared and through the individual contents of belief towards which it had crystallized. Angelus Silesius gives us a foretaste of it, when he separates religious values from all fixed connections with something specific and recognizes their place as lived life.

The Saint when he is drinking
Is also pleasing God
As if he were praying and singing.

He is not concerned, however, with the so-called "secular religion." The latter still clings to determinate contents, which are empirical instead of transcendental. It also channels religious life into specific forms of beauty and greatness, distinction, and lyrical motion. Here, however, religiosity is in question whether it is a direct process of life which encompasses every pulse beat: Is it a being, not a having, is it a form of piousness which is called belief whenever it deals with objects? Now, however, religiosity is similar to life itself. It does not aim to satisfy extrinsic needs, but searches instead for continuous life in a deeper sphere in which it is not yet torn between needs and satisfactions. In this sphere of religious perfection, it does not require an object which prescribes for it a certain form—just as an expressionistic painter does not satisfy his artistic needs by clinging to an exterior subject. Life wishes to express itself directly as religion, not through a language with a given lexicon and prescribed syntax. One could use an apparently paradoxical expression and say: The soul can find faith only by losing it. To preserve the integrity of religious feeling, it must shake off all determined and predetermined religious form.

This desire is often exposed to a form of purely negative criticism which doesn't even understand itself. Nevertheless, it encounters a profound difficulty: life can express itself and realize its freedom only through forms; yet forms must also necessarily suffocate life and obstruct freedom. Piety, or the power of believing, is part of the constitution of the soul, integral to its life: it would influence the soul even in the absence of a religious object—just as an erotic individual must conserve and prove his powers even though he might never meet an object worthy of his love. Nevertheless, I wonder whether the fundamental will of religious life does not require an object, whether a merely functional character and its unformed dynamics which color and bless the mere ups and downs of life—which appear to represent the definitive meaning of so many religious movements—can ever really satisfy it. Perhaps this new religiosity is only a casual interlude. It can be counted among the deepest inner difficulties of numerous modern people that it is impossible to further protect the religions of church tradition, while at the same time the religious drives continue to persist in spite of all "enlightenment." This is so since religion can be robbed only of its clothing but not its life. There is a tempting way out of this dilemma in the cultivation of the religious life as a thing in itself, the transformation of the verb "to believe" from a transitive "I believe that . . ."

to a purely intransitive "I believe." In the long run, perhaps, this might become no less entangled in contradictions. Here again we see the basic conflict inherent in the nature of cultural life. Life must either produce forms or proceed through forms. But forms belong to a completely different order of being. They demand some content above and beyond life; they contradict the essence of life itself, with its weaving dynamics, its temporal fates, the unceasing differentiation of each of its parts. Life is inseparably charged with contradiction. It can enter reality only in the form of its antithesis, that is, only in the form of *form*. This contradiction becomes more urgent and appears more irreconcilable the more life makes itself felt.[1] The forms themselves, however, deny this contradiction: in their rigidly individual shapes, in the demands of their imprescriptible rights, they boldly present themselves as the true meaning and value of our existence. This audacity varies with the degree to which culture has grown.

Life wishes here to obtain something which it cannot reach. It desires to transcend all forms and to appear in its naked immediacy. Yet the processes of thinking, wishing, and forming can only substitute one form for another. They can never replace the form as such by life which as such transcends the form. All these attacks against the forms of our culture, which align against them the forces of life "in itself," embody the deepest internal contradictions of the spirit. Although this chronic conflict between form and life has become acute in many historical epochs, none but ours has revealed it so clearly as its basic theme.

It is a philistine prejudice that conflicts and problems are dreamt up merely for the sake of their solution. Both in fact have additional tasks in the economy and history of life, tasks which they fulfill independently of their own solutions. Thus they exist in their own right, even if the future does not replace conflicts with their resolutions, but only replaces their forms and contents with others. In short, the present is too full of contradictions to stand still. This itself is a more fundamental change than the reformations of times past. The bridge between the past and the future of cultural forms seems to be demolished; we gaze into an abyss of unformed life beneath our feet. But perhaps this formlessness is itself the appropriate form for contemporary life. Thus the blueprint of life is obliquely fulfilled. Life is a struggle in the absolute sense of the term which encompasses the relative contrast between war and peace: that absolute peace which might encompass this contrast remains an eternal (*göttlich*) secret to us.

Note to the Essay

1. Since life is the antithesis of form, and since only that which is somehow formed can be conceptually described, the concept of life cannot be freed from logical imprecision. The essence of life would be denied if one tried to form an exhaustive conceptual definition. In order for conscious life to be fully self-conscious, it would have to do without concepts altogether, for conceptualization inevitably brings on the reign of forms; yet concepts are essential to self-consciousness. The fact that the possibilities of expression are so limited by the essence of life does not diminish its momentum as an idea.

2

On the Concept and the Tragedy
of Culture*

M AN, UNLIKE THE ANIMALS, does not allow himself simply to be
absorbed by the naturally given order of the world. Instead, he
tears himself loose from it, places himself in opposition to it, making demands of it, overpowering it, then overpowered by it. From this first great
dualism springs the never-ending contest between subject and object,
which finds its second round within the realm of spirit itself. The spirit
engenders innumerable structures which keep on existing with a peculiar
autonomy independently of the soul that has created them, as well as
of any other that accepts or rejects them. Thus, man sees himself as
confronting art as well as law, religion as well as technology, science
as well as custom. Now he is attracted, now repelled by their contents,
now fused with them as if they were part of himself, now estranged and
untouched by them. In the form of stability, coagulation, persistent
existence, the spirit becomes object, places itself over against the streaming life, the intrinsic responsibility and the variable tensions of the soul.
Spirit, most deeply tied to spirit, for this very reason experiences innumerable tragedies over this radical contrast: between subjective life,
which is restless but finite in time, and its contents, which, once they
are created, are fixed but timelessly valid.

The concept of culture is lodged in the middle of this dualism. It is
based on a situation which in its totality can only be expressed opaquely,
through an analogy, as the path of the soul to itself. A soul is never

* A translation of "Der Begriff und die Tragödie der Kultur," in Georg Simmel,
Philosophie der Kultur: Gesammelte Essais (Leipzig: Werner Klinkhardt, 1911),
pp. 245–277.

only what it represents at a given moment, it is always "more," a higher and more perfect manifestation of itself, unreal, and yet somehow eternally present. We do not here refer to an ideal mode of being which can be named or fixed at some place within the intellectual world; we mean, rather, the freeing of its self-contained forces of tension, and the development of its innermost core which obeys the intrinsic drive towards form. Just as life—and especially its intensification in consciousness—contains its past history within itself in a more immediate form than does any morsel of the inorganic world. At the same time, this historical element circumscribes its future . . . in a manner which is without analogy in the inorganic realm. The later form of an organism which is capable of growth and procreation is contained in every single phase of organic life. The inner necessity of organic evolution is far profounder than the necessity that a wound-up spring will be released. While everything inorganic contains only the present moment, living matter extends itself in an incomparable way over history and future.

Spiritual movements like *will, duty, hope, the calling* represent psychic expressions of the fundamental destiny of life: to contain its future in its present in a special form which exists only in the life process. Thus the personality as a whole and a unit carries within itself an image, traced as if with invisible lines. This image is its potentiality; to free the image in it would be to attain its full actuality. The ripening and the proving of man's spiritual powers may be accomplished through individual tasks and interests; yet somehow, beneath or above, there stands the demand that through all of these tasks and interests a transcendent promise should be fulfilled, that all individual expressions should appear only as a multitude of ways by which the spiritual life comes to itself. This demand expresses a metaphysical precondition of our practical and emotional existence, however remote it may seem from our real life in the world. It symbolizes a unity which is not simply a formal bond that circumscribes the unfolding of individual powers in an always equal manner, but rather a process of unified development which all individuals go through together. The goal of perfection intrinsically guides the unified development for which all individual capacities and perfections are means.

Here we see the source of the concept of culture, which, however, at this point follows only our linguistic feeling. We are not yet cultivated by having developed this or that individual bit of knowledge or skill; we become cultivated only when all of them serve a psychic unity which depends on but does not coincide with them. Our conscious endeavors aim towards particular interests and potentialities. The development of every human being, when it is examined in terms of identifiable items, appears as a bundle of developmental lines which expand in different directions and quite different lengths. But man does not cultivate himself through their isolated perfections, but only insofar as they help to develop his indefinable personal unity. In other words: Culture is the way that leads from the closed unity through the unfolded multiplicity to the unfolded unity.

This cannot refer only to a development towards something pre-arranged in the germinating forces of personality, sketched out within itself, as a kind of ideal plan. Linguistic usage provides secure guidance here. We will call a garden fruit cultivated which was perfected through the work of a gardener from an inedible tree fruit. Alternately, we might say that this wild tree has been cultivated into a garden fruit tree. But if we were to manufacture a sail mast from the very same tree, even though equally purposive work might be expended upon it, we would not say that the tree had been cultivated into a mast. This nuance of linguistic usage points out that, although the fruit could not have developed from the indigenous powers of the tree without human effort, it only fulfilled the potentialities which were already sketched out in its constitution. This contrasts with the form of the mast, which is superimposed upon the trunk of the tree by a completely alien system of purpose and without any predisposition of its own. It is in this sense that we will not credit a man with genuine culture on the basis of knowledge, virtuosity, or refinements which only act as additives which come to his personality from an external realm of value. In such a case, then, man is the possessor of traits of culture, but he is not cultivated. A man becomes cultivated only when cultural traits develop that aspect of his soul which exists as its most indigenous drive and as the inner predetermination of its subjective perfection.

In this context the conditions finally emerge through which culture resolves the subject-object dualism. We deny the applicability of the concept in the absence of self-development of a psychic center. Nor does the concept apply when this self-development does not depend upon objective and extrinsic means and stations. A multitude of movements can lead the soul to itself. But where as the soul reaches this precept purely from within—in religious ecstasies, moral self-devotion, dominating intellectuality, and harmony of total life—it can still lack the specific property of being cultivated. Not only because it may be lacking that external perfection which in ordinary language is depreciated as mere "civilization." This wouldn't matter at all. The state of being cultivated, however, is not given its purest and deepest meaning when the soul transverses the path from itself to itself, from its poten-tiality to its realization, exclusively on the strength of its subjective powers. Admittedly, when viewed from the highest perspective these processes of perfection are perhaps the most valuable. But this only proves that culture is not the only value for the soul. Its specific meaning, however, is fulfilled only when man includes in this development something which is extrinsic to him, when the path of the soul leads over values which are not themselves of psychic quality. There are objective spiritual forms—art and morality, science and purposively formed objects, religion and law, technology and social norms—stations, as it were, through which the subject has to go in order to gain that special individual value (*Eigenwert*) which is called culture. It is the paradox of culture that subjective life which we feel in its continuous stream and which drives itself towards inner perfection cannot by itself reach the perfection of culture. It can become truly cultivated only through forms which have become completely alien and crystallized into self-sufficient independence. The most decisive way of making this point is to say that culture comes into being by a meeting of the two elements, neither of which contain culture by itself: the subjective soul and the objective spiritual product.

This is the root of the metaphysical significance of historical phenomena. A number of decisive human activities build bridges between subject and object which cannot be completed or which, if completed, are again and again torn down. Some of these are: cognition; above all, work; and in certain of their meanings, also art and religion. The spirit sees itself confronted with an object towards which it is driven by the force as well as spontaneity of its nature. It remains condemned, however, in its own motion, as if in a circle which only touches the object, and which, whenever it is about to penetrate it, is abruptly forced back into its self-contained orbit by the immanent force of its law. The longing for resolution of this intransigent, final dualism is already expressed by the very derivation of the concepts subject-object as correlates, each of which gains its meaning only from the other. Work, art, law, religion, and so forth, transpose the dualism into special atmospheric layers in which its radical sharpness is reduced and certain fusions are permitted. But since these fusions are possible only under special atmospheric conditions, they are unable to overcome the basic estrangement of the parties, and remain finite attempts to solve an infinite task. Our relationship, however, to those objects through which we cultivate ourselves is different, since they themselves are spirit objectified in ethical and intellectual, social and aesthetic, religious and technical forms. The dualism in which a subject restricted to its own boundaries is confronted with an object existing only for itself takes on an incomparable form whenever both parties are spiritual. Thus the subjective spirit has to leave its subjectivity, but not its spirituality, in order to experience the object as a medium for cultivation. This is the only way by which the form of dual existence which is immediately posited with the existence of the subject organizes itself into an inner unified set of mutual relations. Here the subject becomes objective and the object becomes subjective. This is the specific attribute of the process of culture. This process, however, reveals its metaphysical form by transcending its individual contents. In order to understand this more deeply, a further-reaching analysis is required of the objectification of the spirit.

These pages took as their starting point the deep estrangement or animosity which exists between the organic and creative processes of the soul and its contents and products: the vibrating, restless life of the creative soul, which develops toward the infinite contrasts with its fixed and ideally unchanging product and its uncanny feedback effect, which arrests and indeed rigidifies this liveliness. Frequently it appears as if the creative movement of the soul was dying from its own product. Herein lies one fundamental form of our suffering from our own past, our own dogma, and our own fantasies. The discrepancy which exists between the normal states of our inner life and its contents becomes rationalized and somewhat less palpable whenever man, through his theoretical or practical work, confronts himself with these spiritual products, and views them as a sphere of the internal, independent cosmos of the objective spirit. The external or non-material work in which the spiritual life is condensed is perceived as a value of a special kind. Life often goes astray by streaming into it (as if in a blind alley), or continues to roll in its floods and deposits a rejected item at its place. Nevertheless, it is an illustration of the specifically human richness that the products of objective life belong to a stable substantive order of values which is logical or moral, religious or artistic, technical or legal. As carriers of values, their mutual interlocking and systemization frees them from the rigid isolation that alienated them from the rhythms of the processes of life. Thereby this process has gained a significance in its own right which could not have been learned from the steady progression of its course.

Extra value is added to the objectification of the spirit which, although derived in the subjective consciousness, implies by this consciousness something which transcends itself. The value itself does not always need to be positive, in the sense of something good. On the contrary, the merely formal fact that the subject has produced something objective, that its life has become embodied from itself, is perceived as something significant, because the independence of the object thus formed by the spirit can only resolve the basic tension between the process and content of consciousness. Spatially natural ideas attenuate the uncanny fact—that within the flowing process of consciousness something acquires a wholly fixed form—by legitimizing this stability in their relation to an objectively extrinsic world. Objectivity provides the corresponding service for the spiritual world. We feel the very life of our thought tied to the unchangeability of logical norms, the full spontaneity of our actions, to moral norms. The whole process of our consciousness is filled with insights, traditions, and impressions of an environment somehow formed by the spirit. All this rigidity points to a problematic dualism opposed to the restless rhythm of this sub-jective psychic process within which it is generated as imagination and as subjectively psychic content. Insofar as this contrast belongs to an idealized world beyond the (realm of) individual consciousness, it will be reduced to one level and law. It is certainly decisive for the cultural meaning of the object with which we are here concerned that will and intelligence, individuality and feelings, powers and emotions of indi-vidual souls and also of their collectivity are gathered in it. But only where this does go on are those spiritual meanings brought to their destination.

In the happiness of a creator with his work, as great or insignificant as it may be, we find, beyond a discharge of inner tensions, the proof of his subjective power, his satisfaction over a fulfilled challenge, a sense of contentment that the work is completed, that the universe of valuable items is now enriched by this individual piece. Probably there is no higher sublime personal satisfaction for the creator than when we ap-perceive his work in all its impersonality, apart from our subjectivity. Just as the objectifications of the spirit are valuable apart from the subjective processes of life which have produced them, so, too, they have value apart from the other life processes which as their conse-quences depend on them.

As widely and deeply as we look for the influences of the organiza-tion of society, the technical demands of natural phenomena, works of art, and the scientific recognition of truth, custom, and morality, we imply our recognition that these phenomena exist, and that the world also includes this formulation of the spirit. This is a directive, as it were, for our processes of evaluation. It stops with the unique quality of the spiritually objective without questioning spiritual consequences beyond the definition of these items themselves.

In addition to all subjective enjoyments by which a work of art enters into us, we recognize as a value of special kind the fact that the spirit created this vessel for itself. Just as there is at least one line running between the artist's will and the individual property of the work of art, which intertwines his objective evaluation of the work with an enjoyment of his own actively creative force, we find a similarly oriented line in the attitudes of the spectator. These attitudes differ remarkably from our responses to natural phenomena. Ocean and flowers, alpine mountains and the stars in the sky derive what we call their value entirely from their reflections in subjective souls. As soon as we disregard the mystic and fantastic anthropomorphizing of nature, it appears as a continuous contiguous whole, whose undifferentiated character denies its individual parts any special emphasis, any existence which is objectively delimited from others. It is only human categories, that cut out individual parts, to which we ascribe meaning and value. Ironically, we then construct poetic fictions which create a natural beauty that is holy within itself. In reality, however, nature has no other holiness than the one which it evokes in us.

While the product of objective forces can only be subjectively valuable, the product of subjective forces attains for us a kind of objective value. Material and non-material structures which have been invested with human will, artistry, knowledge, and emotions, represent such objective items. We recognize their significance for, and enrichment of, existence, even if we completely disregard the fact that they are being viewed, used, or consumed. Although value and importance, meaning and significance are produced exclusively in the human soul, they must affirm themselves continuously by contrast with the given nature; but this does not harm the objective value of those structures in which those creative human powers and values already have been invested.

A sunrise which is not seen by any human eyes does not increase the value of this world or make it more sublime, since this objective fact by itself is without relevance to the categories of value. As soon, however, as a painter invests his emotion, his sense for form and color and his power of expression, in a picture of this sunrise, then we consider this work an enrichment, an increase in the value of existence as a whole. The world seems to us somehow more deserving of its existence, closer to its ultimate meaning, whenever the human soul, the source of all value has expressed itself in something which has become part of the objective world. It does not matter now whether a later soul will redeem the magic value from the canvas and dissolve it in the stream of his own subjective sensations. Both the sunrise in nature and the painting exist as realities. But where the sunrise attains value only if it lives on in individuals, the painting has already absorbed such life and made it into an object; hence our sense of value stops before it as before something definite which has no need of subjectivization.

If we expand these arguments into a spectrum, one end will show purely subjective life as the source and the locus of all meaning and value. The other extreme will equate value with objectification. It will insist that human life and action are valuable only insofar as they have something tangible to contribute to the idealistic, historical, materialistic cosmos of the spirit. According to this view, even Kant's moral will get its value not in itself, not just by being psychologically "there," but from being embodied in a form which exists in an objectively ideal state. Even sentiments and the personality obtain their significance, in a good or a bad sense, by belonging to a realm of the super-personal.

The subjective and objective spirit are opposed to one another; culture asserts its unity by interpenetrating both. It implies a form of personal perfection which can only be completed through the mediation of a super-personal form which lies outside the subject itself. The specific value being cultivated is inaccessible to the subject unless it is reached through a path of objectively spiritual realities. These again represent *cultural* values only to the extent that they interpenetrate the path of the soul from itself to itself, from what might be called its natural state to its cultivated state.

Hence one can express the structure of the concept of culture in the following terms. There is no cultural value which would be an exclusively cultural value. On the contrary, it must first be a value within some other context, promoting some interest or some capacity of our being. It becomes a cultural value only when this partial development raises our total self one step closer to its perfected unity. It is only in this way that two corresponding situations in intellectual history become intelligible. The first is that men of low cultural interest frequently show remarkable indifference to individual elements of culture, and even reject them—insofar as they fail to discover how these elements can contribute to the fulfillment of their total personalities. (While there is probably no human product which *must* contribute to culture, on the other hand there is probably nothing human that *could not* contribute.) Second, there are phenomena (such as certain formalities and refinements of life) which appear as cultural values only in epochs that have become overripe and tired out. For whenever life itself has become empty and meaningless, developments towards its apex, which are based on the will or its potential, are merely schematic, and not capable of deriving nourishment and promotion from the substantive content of the things and ideas. This is analogous to a sick body which cannot assimilate those substances from food which a healthy body uses for growth and strength. In such a case individual development is capable of deriving from social norms only the socially correct form of conduct, from the arts only unproductive passive pleasures, and from technological progress only the negative aspect of the reduction of effort and the smoothness of daily conduct. The sort of culture that develops is formally subjective, but devoid of interweaving with those substantive elements so essential to culture. On the one hand, there is such an emotionally centralized accentuation of culture that the substantive content of objective factors becomes too much and too diverting, since it thus neither will nor can involve itself into cultural function. On the other hand, there is such a weakness and emptiness of culture that it is not at all capable of including objective factors according to their substantive content. Both these phenomena, which first appear as instances opposed to the link between personal culture and impersonal conditions, thus on closer examination only confirm their connection.

That the final and most decisive factors in life are united in culture becomes especially obvious insofar as the development of each of these factors can occur completely independently, not only without the motivation by the ideal of culture but indeed by denying it. For the view towards one or the other direction would be diverted from the unity of its goal if it were to be determined by a synthesis between these two. The men who produce the constant contents, the objective elements of culture would probably refuse to borrow the motives and values of their efforts directly from the idea of culture. In their case the following inner situation exists: a twofold force is at work in the founder of a religion and in an artist, in a statesman and in an inventor, in a scholar and in a legislator. On the one hand, there is the expression of his essential powers, the exuberation of his nature to such a high level that it frees by itself the contents of cultural life. And on the other hand, there is the passionate dedication to the cause with its immanent laws demanding perfection, so that the creative individual becomes indifferent to himself and is extinguished. Within genius these two streams are unified. To the genius, the development of the subjective spirit for its own sake and compelled by its own forces is indistinguishable from the completely self-negating devotion to an objective task. Culture, as we have demonstrated, is always a synthesis. A synthesis, however, is not the only and most immediate form of unity, since it always presupposes the divisibility of elements as an antecedent or as a correlative.

Viewing synthesis as the most sublime of formal relationships between spirit and world could occur only during an age which is as analytical as the modern. For insofar as the analytic elements are developed in it in ways similar to an organic germ's branching out into a multiplicity of differentiated limbs, this stands beyond analysis and synthesis. This may be so because these two develop from an interaction where each, on every level, presupposes the other, or else because the analytically separated elements are later transformed through synthesis into a unity which, however, is completely different from that which existed prior to the separation. The creative genius possesses such an original unity of the subjective and the objective, which has first to be divided so that it can be resuscitated in synthetic form in the process of cultivation. This is why man's interest in culture does not lie on the same level with pure self-development of the subjective spirit or with pure dedication to a cause; instead cultural interests are attached to a cause, occasionally as something secondary, reflex-like, as an abstract generality which reach beyond the innermost and immediate value impulses of the soul. Even when the path of the soul to itself—one of the primary factors in culture—carries the other factors along, culture stays out of the game as long as the path of the soul transverses only its own domain and perfects itself in the pure self-development of its own essence.

If we consider the other factor of culture in its self-sufficient isolation—those products of the spirit which have grown into an ideal existence independent of all psychological movements—even its most indigenous meaning and value does not coincide with its cultural value. Its cultural meaning is completely independent. A work of art is supposed to be perfect in terms of artistic norms. They do not ask for anything else but themselves, and would give or deny value to the work even if there were nothing else in the world but this particular work. The result of research should be truth and absolutely nothing further. Religion exhausts its meaning with the salvation which it brings to the soul. The economic product wishes to be economically perfect, and does not recognize for itself any other than the economic scale of values. All these sequences operate within the confines of purely internal laws. Whether and to what extent they can be substituted in the development of subjective souls has nothing to do with its importance, which is measured through purely objective norms which are valid for it alone. On the basis of this state of affairs it becomes clear why we frequently meet with an apparent indifference and even aversion to culture among people who are primarily directed only towards subjects as well as among those who are only directed towards objects. A person who asks only for the salvation of the soul, or for the ideal of personal power, or for purely individual growth which will not be affected by any exterior force, will find that his evaluations miss the single *integrating* factor of culture. The other cultural factor will be absent from a person who strives only for the purely material completion of his works, so that they fulfill only their idea and no other that is only tangentially connected. The extreme representative of the first type is the *stylite*, of the other, the specialist who is entrapped by the fanaticism for his specialty. At first sight it is somewhat startling to observe that the supporters of such undoubted "cultural values" as religiosity, personality formation, and technologies of every kind should despise or fight the concept of culture. However, this becomes immediately explicable when we consider that culture always only means the *synthesis* of a subjective development with an objectively spiritual value. It follows then, that the representation of either one of these elements must endanger their mutual interweaving.

This dependence of cultural values on other indigenous value-scales suggests why an object may reach a different point on the scale of cultural values than on that of the merely material. There are a variety of works, which remain far below the artistic, technical, intellectual level of what has already been accomplished, yet which, nevertheless have the capacity to join most efficiently the developmental paths of many people as developers of their latent forces, as a bridge to their next higher station. Just as we do not derive a completely satisfying fulfillment from only the dynamically most forceful or aesthetically most complete impressions of nature (from which we derive the emotional feelings by which stark and unresolved elements suddenly became clear and harmonic to us—which we often owe to a quite simple scene or the playing of shadows on a summer afternoon), so we cannot immediately infer from the importance of the intellectual product, as high or low as it may be in its native dimension, what this work will accomplish for us in the development of culture. Everything depends here on the special significance of the work, which serves as a secondary contribution to the general development of personalities. And this contribution may even be inversely proportional to the unique or intrinsic value of the work.

There are human products of almost ultimate perfection to which we have no access, or they no access to us, because of their perfect integration. Such a work stays in its place, from which it cannot be transplanted to our street as an isolated perfect item. Maybe we can go to it, but we cannot take it along with us in order to raise ourselves through it to our own perfection. For the modern feeling of life this self-contained degree of perfection is, perhaps, represented by antiquity, which denies itself the acceptance of the pulsations and restlessness of our developmental tempo. Many a person may, therefore, be induced today to search for some other fundamental factor especially for our culture. It is similar with certain ethical ideals. Products of the objective intellect which have been so designated are, perhaps, destined more than any others to carry the development from the mere possibility to the highest perfection of our totality and to give it direction.

However, there are some ethical imperatives which contain an ideal of such rigid perfection that it is impossible to draw energies from them which we could include in our development. Despite their high position within the sequence of ethical ideas, as cultural elements they will easily be subordinated to others which from their lower ethical position more readily assimilate themselves into the rhythm of our development. Another reason for the disproportion between the substantive and cultural values of a phenomenon may be found in the one-sided benefits they confer on us. Various things may make us more knowledgeable or better, happier or more adept, without actually helping to develop *us*, but only an independently objective side or quality which is attached to us. In this case we are naturally dealing with gradual and infinitely subtle differences which empirically are hard to grasp, and which are tied to the mysterious relationship between our unified total self and our individual energies and perfections.

The completely closed reality which we call our subject can be designated only by the sum of such individual phenomena, without actually being composed by them. This peculiar relationship is not at all exhausted by reference to the only logical category which is available, the parts and the whole. In isolation it could objectively exist in any number of diverse subjects. It gains the characteristics of our own subjectivity at its inside, where it fosters the growth of the unity of our own being. With these characteristics, however, it somehow builds a bridge to the value of objectivity. It is situated on our periphery by which we are wedded to the objective, exterior, intellectual world. But as soon as this function, which is directed to and nourished by the outside, is severed from its meaning, which flows into our own center, this discrepancy will be created. We will become instructed, we will act more purposively, we will become richer in satisfactions and skills, and perhaps even more educated—our process of cultivation, however, does not keep in step. Although we come from a lower level of having and knowing to a higher level, we do not come from ourselves as lower beings to ourselves as higher beings.

I have stressed the possible discrepancy between the substantive and cultural meaning of an object in order to bring out more emphatically the fundamental duality of elements which through their interweaving produce culture. This interweaving is unique because personal development, although it pertains to the subject, can be reached only through the mediation of objects. For this reason, to be cultivated becomes a task of infinite dimensions, since the number of objects that a subject can make its own is inexhaustible. Nuances of linguistic usage describe this situation most exactly: the word "culture," when it is tied to particular objects, as in religious culture, artistic culture, and so forth, usually designates not the personal qualities of individuals, but rather a general spirit. This means that in any given epoch, there is an especially large number of impressive spiritual products available through which individuals are cultivated. But this plenitude of cultural possibilities may actually constitute a threat to culture, if it leads to over-specialization. A person may acquire a remarkable degree of skill or knowledge concerning a certain substantive content—an "artistic culture" or a "religious culture"—without becoming truly cultivated. On the other hand, it is still possible that substantive perfection of a particular kind may help bring about the completion of the person as a total being.

Within this structure of culture there now develops a cleavage which, of course, is already prepared in its foundation. It makes of the subject-object-synthesis a paradox, even a tragedy. The profound dualism between subject and object survives their synthesis. The inner logic by which each member develops independently does not necessarily coincide with that of the other. Knowledge, for example, whose forms are so greatly determined by the *a priori* dimensions of our spirit, is constantly becoming completed by items which can be only accepted and not anticipated. But it does not seem to be guaranteed that these items will serve the completion of the soul. It is similar with our practical and technical relationships to things; although we form them according to our purposes, they do not yield to us completely, but have a logic and a power of their own. And it is highly doubtful that our use of them will always coincide with the unique direction of our central development. Indeed, everything objective possesses its own individual logic. Once certain themes of law, of art, of morals have been created —even if they have been created by most individual and innermost spontaneity—we cannot control the directions in which they will develop. Although we generate them, they must follow the guidelines of their own inner necessity, which is no more concerned with our individuality than are physical forces and their laws.

It is true that language rhymes and reasons for us; it collects the fragmentary impulses of our own essence and leads them to a perfection which we would not have reached on our own. Nevertheless, there is no necessity in the parallel between objective and subjective developments. Indeed, we sometimes even perceive language as a strange natural force which deflects and mutilates not only our expressions, but also our most intimate intentions. And religion, which originated in the search of the soul for itself, analogous to wings that carry the indigenous forces of the soul to their own height—it, too, has certain formative laws, which having once come into existence, unfold with a necessity that does not always coincide with our own. The anti-cultural spirit with which religion is often reproached is not only its occasional animosity toward intellectual, aesthetic, or moral values. It also refers to the deeper issue that religion proceeds on its own course, which is determined by immanent logic, and into which it drags life along. Whatever transcendental fulfillment the soul may find on this course, religion rarely leads to that perfection of its totality which is called culture.

Insofar as the logic of impersonal cultural forms is loaded with dynamic tensions, harsh frictions develop between these forms and the inner drives and norms of personality which fulfill themselves in culture. From the moment that man began to say "I" to himself, and became an object beyond and in comparison with himself, from the same moment in which the contents of the soul were formed together into a center point—from that time and based on that central form the ideal had to grow according to which everything connected with the center point formed a unit, self-contained and self-sufficient. But the contents with which the "I" must organize itself into its own unified world do not belong to it alone. They are given to it from some spatially, temporarily idealized realm outside; they are simultaneously the contents of different social and metaphysical, conceptual and ethical worlds.

In these they possess forms and relationships among one another that do not wish to dissolve into those of the "I." Through those contents the exterior worlds grasp the "I" and seek to draw it into them. They aim to break up the centralization of cultural contents around the "I" and reconstitute them according to *their* demands. Thus, in religious conflicts between the self-sufficiency or freedom of man and his subordination under divine order, and again in social conflicts between man as a rounded individual and man as a mere member of a social organism, we are entangled because our life ideals are inevitably subsumed under other circles than those of our own "I."

Man often finds himself at the point of intersection of two circles of objective forces and values, each of which would like to drag him along. Often he feels himself to be the center who orders all life contents around himself harmonically according to the logic of his personality. Thus he feels solidarity with each of these circles, insofar as each belongs to a different circle, and is claimed by another law of motion, his own. Thus our own essence forms an intersecting point of itself with an alien circle of postulates. The process of culture, however, compresses the parties of this collision into extremely close contact by making the development of the subject conditional on the assimilation of objective material. Thus the metaphysical dualism of subject and object, which seemed to have been overcome by the formation of culture, reappears in the conflict between subjective and objective developments. It is possible, moreover, that the object can step outside its mediating role in an even more basic manner, and break up the bridges over which the course of cultivation has been leading. At first it isolates and alienates itself from the working subject through the division of labor. Objects which have been produced by many persons can be arranged in a scale according to the extent to which their unity stems from the unified intellectual intention of one person, or from the partial contributions of cooperating but uncomprehending individuals. The latter pole is occupied by a city: it may strike us now as a meaningful self-contained and organically connected whole; in fact, however, it was not constructed according to any pre-existing plan, but arose out of the accidental needs and desires of individuals. The former pole is exemplified by the products of a manufacturing plant in which twenty workers have cooperated without knowledge of or interest in one another's separate work processes—while the whole, nevertheless, has been guided by a personal central will and intellect. An intermediary position is taken by a newspaper, insofar as its overall appearance can somehow be traced to a leading personality, and yet it grows because of mutually accidental contributions of the most diverse form and of diverse individuals who are complete strangers to one another. Through the cooperative effort of different persons, then, a cultural object often comes into existence which as a total unit is *without a producer*, since it did not spring forth from the total self of any individual. The elements are coordinated as if by a logic and formal intention inherent in them as objective realities; their creators have not endowed them with any such logic and intention. The objectivity of the spiritual content, which makes it independent of its acceptance or non-acceptance can be attributed here to the production process. Regardless of whether they were or were not intended by individuals, the finished product contains contents which can be transmitted through the cultural process. This is different only in degree from a little child who, in playing with letters of the alphabet, may order them accidentally into good sense. The meaning exists objectively and concretely, no matter how naively it may have been produced.

If examined more closely, this appears as an extremely radical case of an otherwise general human-spiritual fate. Most products of our intellectual creation contain a certain quota which was not produced by ourselves. I do not mean unoriginality or the inheritance of values or dependence on traditional examples. Even despite of all these, a given work in its total content could still be born in our own consciousness although the consciousness would thus only hand on what it had already received. On the contrary, there is always something significant in most of our objective efforts which other people can extract even though we were not aware of having deposited it there. In some sense it is valid to say that the weaver doesn't know what he weaves. The finished effort contains emphases, relationships, values which the worker did not intend. It is mysterious but unquestionably true: a material object takes on a spiritual meaning not put into it but integral to the object's form. Nature does not present this sort of problem. It is not the will of any artist that has given purity of style to the southern mountains, or gripping symbolism to a stormy ocean. The realm of the purely natural is endowed with the potential for meaning: it has or can have a part in all intellectual creations. The possibility of gaining a subjectively intellectual content is invested in them as an objective form. In an extreme example, a poet may have coined a puzzle with the intention of a certain solution. If, now, a different solution is found for it which fits as well, as meaningfully, as the intended one, then it will be exactly as "right" even though it was absolutely alien to his creative processes. It is contained within the created product as an idealized objectivity exactly as is the first word for which the puzzle originally had been created.

These potentialities of the objective spirit show that it possesses an independent validity, an independent chance of becoming re-subjectivized after its successful objectification, even when it was created by a subjective spirit. This chance, however, does not need to be realized: in the previous example, the second solution to the puzzle rightfully exists in its objective meaning even before it is found, indeed, even if it is never found. This peculiarity of the contents of culture is the metaphysical foundation for the ominous independence by which the realm of cultural products grows and grows as if an inner necessity were producing one member after another. Frequently this happens almost without relation to the will and personality of the producer and independent of the acceptance by consumers.

The "fetishism" which Marx assigned to economic commodities represents only a special case of this general fate of contents of culture. With the increase in culture these contents more and more stand under a paradox: they were originally created by subjects and for subjects: but in their intermediate form of objectivity, which they take on in addition to the two extreme instances, they follow an immanent logic of development. In so doing they estrange themselves from their origin as well as from their purpose. They are impelled not by physical necessities, but by truly cultural ones (which, however, cannot pass over the physical conditions). What drives forth the products of the spirit is the cultural and not the natural scientific logic of the objects. Herein lies the fatefully immanent drive of all technology, as soon as it has moved beyond the range of immediate consumption. Thus the industrial production of a variety of products generates a series of closely related by-products for which, properly speaking, there is no need. It is only the compulsion for full utilization of the created equipment that calls for it. The technological process demands that it be completed by links which are not required by the psychic process. Thus vast supplies of products come into existence which call forth an artificial demand that is senseless from the perspective of the subjects' culture.

In several branches of the sciences it is no different. On one hand, for example, philological techniques have developed to an unsurpassable finesse and methodological perfection. On the other hand, the study of subject matter which would be of genuine interest to intellectual culture does not replenish itself as quickly. Thus, the philological effort frequently turns into micrology, pedantic efforts, and an elaboration of the unessential into a method that runs on for its own sake, an extension of substantive norms whose independent path no longer coincides with that of culture as a completion of life. The same problem arises in the development of fine arts, where technical skills have developed to such an extent that they are emancipated from serving the cultural total purpose of art. By obeying only the indigenous material logic, the technique at this point develops refinement after refinement. However, these refinements represent only *its* perfection, no longer the cultural meaning of art. That extreme and total specialization—of which there are complaints nowadays in all areas of labor, but which nevertheless subordinates their progress under its laws with demonical rigor—is only a special form of this very general cultural predicament. Objects, in their development, have a logic of their own—not a conceptual one, nor a natural one, but purely as cultural works of man; bound by their own laws, they turn away from the direction by which they could join the personal development of human souls. This is not that old familiar intrusion of the realm of ultimate ends, not the primacy of technique so often lamented in advanced cultures. That is something purely psychological, without any firm relationship to the objective order of things. Here, however, we are dealing with the immanent logic of cultural phenomena. Man becomes the mere carrier of the force by which this logic dominates their development and leads them on as if in the tangent of the course through which they would return to the cultural development of living human beings—this is similar to the process by which because of strict adherence to logic our thoughts are lead into theoretical consequences which are far removed from those originally intended. This is the real tragedy of culture.

In general we call a relationship tragic—in contrast to merely sad or extrinsically destructive—when the destructive forces directed against some being spring forth from the deepest levels of this very being; or when its destruction has been initiated in itself, and forms the logical development of the very structure by which a being has built its own positive form. It is the concept of culture that the spirit creates an independent objectivity by which the development of the subject takes its path. In this process the integrating and culturally conditioning element is restricted to an unique evolution which continues to use up the powers of other subjects, and to pull them into its course without thereby raising them to their own apex. The development of subjects cannot take the same path which is taken by that of the objects. By following the latter, it loses itself either in a dead end alley or in an emptiness of its innermost and most individual life. Cultural development places the subject even more markedly outside of itself through the formlessness and boundlessness which it imparts to the objective spirit, because of the infinite number of its producers. Everybody can contribute to the supply of objectified cultural contents without any consideration for other contributors. This supply may have a determined color during individual cultural epochs that is, from within there may be a qualitative but not likewise quantitative boundary. There is no reason why it should not be multiplied in the direction of the infinite, why not book should be added to book, work of art to work of art, or invention to invention. The form of objectivity as such possesses a boundless capacity for fulfillment. This voracious capacity for accumulation is most deeply incompatible with the forms of personal life. The receptive capacity of the self is limited not only by the force and length of life, but also through a certain unity and relative compactness of its form. Therefore, the self selects, with determined limits from among the contents which offer themselves as means for its individual development. The individual might pass by what his self-development cannot assimilate, but this does not always succeed so easily. The infinitely growing supply of objectified spirit places demands before the subject, creates desires in him, hits him with feelings of individual inadequacy and helplessness, throws him into total relationships from whose impact he cannot withdraw, although he cannot master their particular contents. Thus, the typically problematic situation of modern man comes into being: his sense of being surrounded by an innumerable number of cultural elements which are neither meaningless to him nor, in the final analysis, meaningful. In their mass they depress him, since he is not capable of assimilating them all, nor can he simply reject them, since after all, they do belong *potentially* within the sphere of his cultural development. This could be characterized with the exact reversal of the words that refer to the first Franciscan monks in their spiritual poverty, their absolute freedom from all things which wanted to divert the path of their souls: *Nihil habentes, omnia possidentes* (those who have nothing own everything). Instead man has become richer and more overloaded: *Cultures omnia habentes, nihil possidentes* (cultures which have everything own nothing).

These experiences have already been discussed in various forms.

(I have elaborated them in my *Philosophy of Money* for a larger number of concrete historical fields.) What we want to bring out here is their deep roots in the concept of culture. The total wealth of this concept consists in the fact that objective phenomena are included in the process of development of subjects, as ways or means, without thereby losing their objectivity. Whether this does in fact bring the subject to the highest degree of perfection may remain an open question. In any case, the metaphysical intention which attempts to unify the principles of the subject and of the object finds here a guarantee of its success: the metaphysical question finds an historical answer. In cultural forms, the spirit reaches an objectivity which makes it at once independent of all accidents of subjective reproductions, and yet usable for the central purpose of subjective perfection. While the metaphysical answers to this question in general tend to cut it off by somehow demonstrating that the subject-object contrast is unimportant, culture insists on the full opposition of the parties, on the super-subjective logic of spiritually formed objects through which the subject raises itself beyond itself to itself.

One of the basic capacities of the spirit is to separate itself from itself—to create forms, ideas and values that oppose it, and only in this form to gain consciousness of itself. This capacity has reached its widest extent in the process of culture. Here the spirit has pressed the object most energetically towards the subject, in order to lead it back into the subject. But this liaison dissolves because of the object's indigenous logic, through which the subject regains itself as more adequate and perfected. The tendency of creative people to think not about the cultural value of their work, but about its substantive meaning which is circumscribed by its unique idea, develops logically but almost imperceptibility into caricature, into a form of specialization which is secluded from life, into a purely technical (and technological) self-satisfaction which does not find its path back to man. This objectivity makes possible the division of labor, which collects the energies of a whole complex of personalities in a single product, without considering whether individuals will be able to use it for their own development, or whether it will satisfy only extrinsic and peripheral needs. Herein lies the deeper rationale for the ideals of Ruskin to replace all factory labor by the artistic labor of individuals.

The division of labor separates the product as such from each individual contributor. Standing by itself, as an independent object, it is suitable to subordinate itself into an order of phenomena, or to serve an individual's purposes. Thereby, however, it loses that inner animation which can only be given to a total work by a complete human being, which carries its usefulness into the spiritual center of other individuals. A work of art is such an immeasurable cultural value

45

precisely because it is inaccessible to any division of labor, because the created product preserves the creator to the innermost degree.

What in Ruskin's work might appear as a hatred of culture in reality is a passion for culture. He wants to reverse the division of labor which, by emptying cultural content of its subject, and giving it an inanimate objectivity, tears it from the genuinely cultural process. The tragic development which ties culture to the objectivity of contents, but charges the contents with a logic of their own, and thus withdraws them from cultural assimilation by subjects, is now evident to everyone who observes the infinite potential for multiplying the contents of the objective spirit at random. Since culture does not possess a concrete unity of form for its contents, and since each creator places his product as if in an unbounded space next to that of the other, the mass character of phenomena comes into existence. Everything claims with a certain right to be of cultural value, and creates in us a wish thus to utilize it. The lack of unity in the objectified spirit permits it a developmental tempo behind which the subjective spirit must increasingly lag. The subjective spirit, meanwhile, does not know how it can completely protect its unity of form from the touch and the temptation of all these "things." The superior force of the object over the subject, so general in the course of the world, temporarily checked by the fortunate balance we call culture, can once again be felt as the objective spirit develops unboundedly. The adornment and overloading of our lives with a thousand superfluous items, from which, however, we cannot liberate ourselves; the continuous "stimulation" of civilized man who in spite of all this is not stimulated to expressions of individual creativity; the more acquaintance with or enjoyment of a thousand things which our development cannot include and which stay in it only as ballast—all these long-lamented cultural ills are nothing more than reflections of the emancipation of the objectified spirit. Thus cultural contents are bound to follow a logic which eventually is independent of their *cultural purpose*, and which continuously leads them further away from it. The situation is tragic: even in its first moments of existence, culture carries something within itself which, as if by an intrinsic fate, is determined to block, to burden, to obscure and divide its innermost purpose, the transition of the soul from its incomplete to its complete state.

The great enterprise of the spirit succeeds innumerable times in overcoming the object as such by making an object of itself, returning to itself enriched by its creation. But the spirit has to pay for this self-perfection with the tragic potential that a logic and dynamic is inevitably created by the unique laws of its own world which increasingly separates the contents of culture from its essential meaning and value.

3

A Chapter in the Philosophy of Value*

T HE FACT OF ECONOMIC EXCHANGE confers upon the value of things something super-individual. It detaches them from dissolution in the mere subjectivity of the agents, and causes him to determine each other reciprocally, since each exerts its economic function in the other. The practically effective value is conferred upon the object, not merely by its own desirability, but by the desirability of another object. Not merely the relationship to the receptive subjects characterizes this value, but also the fact that it arrives at this relationship only at the price of a sacrifice; while from the opposite point of view this sacrifice appears as a good to be enjoyed, and the object in question, on the contrary, as a sacrifice. Hence the objects acquire a reciprocity of counterweight, which makes value appear in a quite special manner as an objective quality indwelling in themselves. While the object itself is the thing in controversy—which means that the sacrifice which it represents is being determined—its significance for both contracting parties appears much more as something outside of these latter and self-existent than if the individual thought of it only in its relation to himself. We shall see later how also isolated industry, by placing the workman over against the demands of nature, imposes upon him the like necessity of sacrifice for gaining of the object, so that in this case also the like relationship, with the one exception that only a single party has been changed, may endow the object with the same independent qualities, yet with their significance dependent upon its own objective conditions. Desire and the feeling of the agent stand, to be sure, as the motor energy behind all this, but from this in and of itself this value form

* Reprinted from *The American Journal of Sociology*, V (5): 577–603, 1900. The translation corresponds closely to Part II of Chapter 1 of the 1907 edition of *Philosophie des Geldes*.

could not proceed. It rather comes only from the reciprocal counterbalancing of the objects.

To be sure, in order that equivalence and exchange of values may emerge, some material to which value can attach must be at the basis. For industry as such the fact that these materials are equivalent to each other and exchangeable is the turning point. It guides the stream of appraisal through the form of exchange, at the same time creating a middle realm between desires, in which all human movement has its source, and the satisfaction of enjoyment in which it culminates. The specific character of economic activity as a special form of commerce exists, if we may venture the paradox, not so much in the fact that it exchanges *values* as that it *exchanges* values. To be sure, the significance which things gain in and with exchange never rests isolated by the side of their subjective immediate significance, that is, the one originally decisive of the relationship. It is rather the case that the two belong together, as form and content connote each other. But the objective procedure makes an abstraction, so to speak, from the fact that values constitute its material, and derives its peculiar character from the equality of the same—somewhat as geometry finds its tasks only in connection with the magnitude-relations of things, without bringing into its consideration the substances in connection with which alone these relationships actually have existence. That thus not only reflection upon industry, but industry itself, consists, so to speak, in a real abstraction from the surrounding actuality of the appraising processes is not so wonderful as it at first appears when we once make clear to ourselves how extensively human practice, cognition included, reckons with abstractions. The energies, relationships, qualities of things—to which in so far as our own proper essence also belongs—constitute objectively a unified interrelationship, which is divided into a multiplicity of independent series or motives only after the interposition of our interests, and in order to be manipulated by us. Accordingly, each science investigates phenomena which possess an exclusive unity, and clean-cut lines of division from the problems of other sciences, only from the point of view which the special science proposes as its own. Reality, on the other hand, has no regard to these boundary lines, but every section of the world presents a conglomeration of tasks for the most numerous sciences. Likewise, our practice dissects one-sided series from the external or internal complexity of things. Notice, for example, into how many systems a forest is divided. These in turn become objects of special interest to a hunter, a proprietor, a poet, a painter, a civic official, a botanist, and a tourist. The forest is objectively always the same. It is a real, indivisible unity of all the determinations and relationships out of which the interested parties each select a certain group, and make it into a picture of the forest. The same is the case with the great systems of interest of which a civilization is composed. We distinguish, for instance, interests and relationships as the ethical, the egoistic, the economic, the domestic, etc. The reciprocal weaving together of these constitutes actual life. Certain of these, however, dissociated from this concrete reality, constitute the content of the civic structure. The state is an abstraction of energies and reciprocal actions which, in the concrete, exist only within a unity that is not separable into its parts. Again, in like manner, pedagogy abstracts from the web of cosmic contents certain items into the totality of which the pupil is subsequently to enter, and forms them into a world which is completely abstract, in comparison with reality. In this world the pupil is to live. To what extent all art runs a division line of its own through the conditions of things, in addition to those that are traced out in the real structure of the objective world, needs no elaboration. In opposition to that naturalism which wanted to lead art away from the selective abstraction, and to open to it the whole breadth and unity of reality, in which all elements have equally rights, in so far as they are actual—precisely in opposition to this has criticism shown the complete impracticability of the tendency; and that even the extremest purpose, to be satisfied in art only with undifferentiated completeness of the object, must at last end in an abstraction. It will merely be the product of another selective principle. Accordingly, this is one of the formulas in which we may express the relation of man to the world, viz., from the unity and the interpenetration of things in which each bears the other and all have equal rights. Our practice, no less than our theory, constantly abstracts isolated elements, and forms them into unities relatively complete in themselves. Except in quite general feelings, we have no relationship to the totality of being. Only when in obedience to the necessities of our thought and action we derive perpetual abstractions from phenomena, and endow these with the relative independence of a merely subjective coherence to which the continuity of the world-movement as objective gives no room, do we reach a relationship to the world that is definite in its details. Indeed, we may adopt a scale of values for our culture systems, according to the degree in which they combine the demands of our singular purposes with the possibility of passing over without a gap from each abstraction which they present to the other, so that a subsequent combination is possible which approximates that objective coherence and unity. Accordingly, the economic system of the world is assuredly founded upon an abstraction, that is, upon the relation of reciprocity and exchange, the balance between sacrifice and gain; while in the actual process in which this takes place it is inseparably amalgamated with its foundations and its results, the desires and the satisfactions. But this form of existence does not distinguish it from the other territories into which, for the purposes of our interests, we subdivide the totality of phenomena.

The objectivity of economic value which we assume as defining the scope of economics, and which is thought as the independent characteristic of the same in distinction from its subjective vehicles and consequences, consists in its being true of many, or rather all, subjects. The decisive factor is its extension in principle beyond the individual. The fact that for one object another must be given shows that not merely for me, but also for itself, that is, also for another person, the object is of some value. The appraisal takes place in the form of economic value.

The exchange of objects, moreover, in which this objectivication, and therewith the specific character of economic activity, realizes itself belongs, from the standpoint of each of the contracting parties, in the quite general category of gain and loss, purpose and means. If any object over which we have control is to help us to the possession or enjoyment of another, it is generally under the condition that we forego the enjoyment of its own peculiar worth. As a rule the purpose consumes either the substance or the force of the means, so that the value of the same constitutes the price which must be paid for the value of the purpose. As a rule, only within certain spiritual interests is that not the case. The mind has been properly compared to a fire, in which countless candles may be lighted without loss of its own peculiar intensity. For example, intellectual products sometimes (not always) retain for purposes of instruction their own worth, which does not lose any of its independent energy and significance by functioning as means to the pedagogical end. In the case of causal series in external nature, however, the relationship is usually different. Here must the object, if it is conceived on the one hand as immediately valuable, and on the other hand, as means to the attainment of another value, be sacrificed as a value in itself, in order to perform its office as means. This procedure rules all values the enjoyment of which is connected with a conscious action on our part. What we call exchange is obviously nothing but a special case of this typical form in human life. We must regard this, however, not merely as a placing of exchange in the universal category of creation of value; but, conversely, this latter as an exchange in the wider sense of the word. This possibility, which has so many consequences for the theory of value, will become clear by the discussion of the doctrine that all economic value consists in exchange value.

To this theory the objection has been made that even the quite isolated economic man—he who neither sells nor buys—must estimate his products and means of production according to their value, if expenditures and results are to stand in proper relation to each other. This objection, however, is not so striking as it appears, for all consideration whether a definite product is worth enough to justify a definite expenditure of labor or other goods is, for the economic agent, precisely the same as the appraisal which takes place in connection with exchange. In confronting the concept "exchange" there is frequently the confusion of ideas which consists in speaking of a relationship as though it were something apart from the elements between which it plays. It means, however, only a condition or a change within each of these elements. There is nothing between them in the sense of a spatial object that can be distinguished in space between two other objects. When we compose the two acts or changes of condition which in reality take place into the notion "exchange," the conception is attractive that something has happened in addition to or beyond that which took place in each of the contracting parties. Considered with reference to its immediate content, exchange is nothing but the twofold repetition of the fact that an actor now has something which he previously did not have, and on the other hand does not have something which he previously had. That being the case, the isolated economic man, who surely must make a sacrifice to gain certain products, acts precisely like the one who makes exchanges. The only difference is that the party with whom he contracts is not a second sentient being, but the natural order and regularity of things, which no more satisfy our desires without a sacrifice on our part than would another person. His appraisals of value, in accordance with which he governs his actions, are, as a rule, precisely the same as in the case of exchange; for the economic actor, as such, it is surely quite immaterial whether the substances or labor energies in his possession are sunk in the ground or given to another man, if only there accrues to him the same result from the sacrifice. This subjective process of sacrifice and gain in the individual soul is by no means something secondary or imitative in comparison with inter-individual exchange; on the contrary, the give-and-take between sacrifice and accomplishment, within the individual, is the basal presumption, and at the same time the persistent substance, of every two-sided exchange. The latter is merely a sub-species of the former; that is, the sort in which the sacrifice is occasioned by the demand of another individual. At the same time, it can only be occasioned by the same sort of result for the actor so far as objects and their qualities are concerned. It is of extreme importance to make this reduction of the economic process to that which actually takes place, that is, in the soul of every economic agent. We must not allow ourselves to be deceived about the essential thing by the fact that in the case of exchange this process is reciprocal—that is, that it is conditioned by the

51

like procedure in another. The main thing is that the natural and solitary economic transaction, if we may conceive of such a thing, runs back to the same fundamental form as two-sided exchange, to the process of equalization between two subjective occurrences within the individual. This is in its proper essence not affected by the secondary question whether the impulse to the process proceeds from the nature of things or the nature of man, whether it is a matter of purely natural economy or of exchange economy. All feelings of value, in other words, which are set free by producible objects are in general to be gained only by foregoing other values. At the same time, such sacrifice may consist, not only in that mediate labor for ourselves which appears as labor for others, but frequently enough in that quite immediate labor for our own personal purposes.

Moreover, those theories of value which discover in labor the absolute element of value accommodate themselves to this form of conception as to the higher and more abstract idea. Whoever labors sacrifices something which he possesses—his labor-power, or his leisure, or his pleasure merely in the self-satisfying play of his powers—in order to get in exchange for these something which he does not possess. Through the fact that labor accomplishes this, it acquires value, just as, on the other side, the attained object is valuable for the reason that it has cost labor. In so far there is not the slightest ground to give labor a special position as contrasted with all other conditions of value. The difference between these is only of a quantitative nature. Labor is the most frequent object of exchange. In this assertion we forbear to enter into the discussion whether labor or labor power, and in what form, constitute an object of exchange. Because labor is regarded as a sacrifice, as something painful, it is performed only when an object can be secured by it which corresponds to the eudæmonistic or some other demand. If labor were nothing but pleasure, the products that it wrings from nature would have no value whatever, provided we disregard the difference in abundance of objects. On the contrary, if objects that satisfy our desires came to us of their own accord, labor would have no more value. Thus on the whole we may say that, considered from the standpoint of value, every economic transaction is an exchange, and every single article of value furnishes its additional quota to the total value of life only after deduction of a certain sacrificed quantum of value.

In all the foregoing it is presupposed that a definite scale of value exists in the case of the objects, and that each of the two objects concerned in the transaction signifies, for the one contracting party the desired gain, for the other the necessary sacrifice. But this presumption is, as a matter of fact, much too simple. If, as is necessary, we regard economic activity as a special case of the universal life form of exchange, as a sacrifice in return for a gain, we shall from the beginning suspect something of what takes place within this form, namely, that the value of the gain is not, so to speak, brought with it, ready-made, but it accrues to the desired object, in part or even entirely, through the measure of the sacrifice demanded in acquiring it. These cases, which are as frequent as they are important for the theory of value, seem to harbor an essential contradiction, to be sure, for they require us to make a sacrifice of value for things which in themselves are worthless. As a matter of course, no one would forego value without receiving for it at least equal value; and, on the contrary, that the end should receive its value only through the price that we must give, for it could be the case only in a crazy world. This is now, for immediate consciousness, correct. Indeed, it is more correct than that popular standpoint is apt to allow in other cases. As a matter of fact, the value which an actor surrenders for another value can never be greater for this actor himself, under the actual circumstances of the moment, than the one for which it is given. All contrary appearances rest upon confusion of the value actually estimated by the actor with the value which the object of exchange in question usually has. For instance, when one at the point of death from hunger offers a jewel for a piece of bread, he does it only because the latter, under the given circumstances, is of more value to him than the former. Particular circumstances, however, are necessary in order to attach to an object a valuation, for every such valuation is an incident of the whole complex system of our feelings, which is in constant flux, adaptation, and reconstruction. Whether these circumstances are exceptional or relatively constant is obviously in principle a matter of indifference. There can be no doubt, at any rate, that in the moment of the exchange, that is, of the making of the sacrifice, the value of the exchanged object forms the limit which is the highest point to which the value of the sacrificed object can rise. Quite independent of this is the question whence that former object derives its so necessary value, and whether it may come from the objects that are to be sacrificed for it, so that the equivalence between gain and price would be established at once *a posteriori*, and by the latter. We shall see presently how often value comes into existence, psychologically, in this apparently illogical manner. If, however, it is once in existence, the psychological necessity exists in its case, not less than in that of value constituted in any other way, of regarding it as a positive good at least equal to the negative good sacrificed for it. In fact, there is a series of cases in which the sacrifice not merely raises the value of the aim, but even produces it. It is the joy of exertion, of overcoming difficulties, frequently indeed that of contradiction, which expresses itself in this process. The necessary detour to the attainment of certain things is often the occasion, often also the cause, of regarding them as valuable. In the relationships of men to each other, most frequently and evidently in erotic relations, we notice how reserve, indifference, or repulse inflames the most passionate desire to conquer in spite of these obstacles, and spurs us to efforts and sacrifices which, without these obstacles, would surely seem to us excessive. For many people the æsthetic results of ascending the high Alps would not be considered worth further notice, if it did not demand extraordinary effort and danger, and if it did not thereby acquire tone, attractiveness, and consecration. The charm of antiquities and curiosities is frequently no other. If no sort of æsthetic or historical interest attaches to them, a substitute for it is furnished by the mere difficulty of acquiring them. They are worth just what they cost. This, then, appears secondarily to mean that they cost what they are worth. Furthermore, all moral merit signifies that for the sake of the morally desirable deed contrary impulses and wishes must be fought down and sacrificed. If the act occurs without any conquest, as the matter-of-course outflow of unrestrained impulse, it is not appraised so high in the scale of subjective moral value, however desirable objectively its content may be. In this latter case we are not moral in any sense other than the flower is beautiful; we do not reckon the beauty of the flower as an ethical merit. Only through the sacrifice of the lower and still so seductive good is the height of moral merit attained, and a more lofty height, the more attractive the temptation and the deeper and more comprehensive the sacrifice. We might array illustrations, beginning with the ordinary selfishness of the day, the overcoming of which alone rewards us with the consciousness of being somewhat worthy, and rising to that force of logic whose sacrifice in favor of belief in the absurd seemed to the schoolmen an extreme religious merit. If we observe which human achievements attain to the highest honors and appraisals, we find it to be always those which betray a maximum of humility, effort, persistent concentration of the whole being, or at least seem to betray these. In other words, they seem to manifest the most self-denial, sacrifice of all that is subsidiary, and devotion of the subjective to the objective ideal. And if, in contrast with all this, æsthetic production and everything easy, inviting, springing from the naturalness of impulse, unfolds an incomparable charm, this owes its special quality still to the undefined feeling of the burdens and sacrifices which are usually the condition of gaining such things. The mobility and inexhaustible power of combination of our mental content frequently brings it about that the significance of a correlation is carried over to its direct converse, somewhat as the association between two ideas occurs equally when they are asserted or denied of each other. The specific value of anything which we gain without conquered difficulty and as the gift of fortunate accident is felt by us only on the ground of the significance which the things have for us that are gained with difficulty and measured by sacrifice. It is the same value, but with the negative sign, and this is the primary from which the other may be derived; but the reverse is not the case.

If we look for an occurrence of this relationship within the economic realm, it seems to be demanded, in the first place, that we shall in thought separate the economic element, as a specific difference or form, from the fact of value as the universality of the substance of the same. If for the present we take value as a datum, and not now to be discussed, it is at least, in accordance with all the foregoing, not doubtful that economic value as such does not accrue to an object in its isolated self-existence, but only through the employment of another object which is given for it. Wild fruit picked without effort, and not given in exchange, but immediately consumed, is no economic good. It can count as such only when its consumption saves some other sort of economic expense. If, however, all the demands of life were to be satisfied in this fashion, so that no sacrifice was at any point necessary, men would simply not engage in industry, any more than do the birds or the fishes, or the denizens of fairyland. Whatever be the way in which the two objects, A and B, came to have value, A came to have an *economic* value only through the fact that I must give B for it, B only through the fact that I can receive A for it. In this case, as above stated, it is in principle indifferent whether the sacrifice takes place by means of the transfer of a thing of value to another person, that is, through inter-individual exchange, or within the circle of the individual's own interests, through a balancing of efforts and results. In the articles of commerce there is nothing to be found but the significance which each has, directly or indirectly, for our need to consume, and the give-and-take that occurs between them. Since, now, as we have seen, the former does not of itself suffice to make the given object an object of economic activity, it follows that the latter alone can supply to it the specific difference which we call economic.

If thus, under the preliminary assumption of an existing value, the economic character of the same coincides with the offer of another object for it, and of it for the other object, there arises the further question whether this separation between the value and its economic form is necessary and possible. As a matter of fact, this artificially dividing abstraction finds in reality no counterpart. In the economic value the economic is as little sundered from the value as in the economic man the economist is sundered from the man. To be sure, man is possible in times and relations in which he does not pursue economic activity. The latter, however, is not possible without being accomplished by men, in absolute unity with them, and only in unreal conceptual abstraction is it to be sundered from them. Thus there are enough objects of value which are not economic, but there are no objects of economic value which are not also valuable in every relation in which they are economic. What is true of the economic as such is, therefore, true of the values of industry, as every condition or quality or function is necessarily a condition or quality or function of that general object to which this quality or function pertains. The economic form of the value stands between two boundaries: on the one hand, the desire for the object, which attaches itself to the anticipated feeling of satisfaction from its possession and enjoyment; on the other hand, to this enjoyment itself, which, exactly considered, is not an economic act. That is, as soon as we concede that immediate consumption of wild fruits is not an economic procedure, and therefore the fruits themselves have no economic value (except in so far as they save the production of economic values), then the consumption of values properly economic is no longer economic, for the act of consumption, in this last case, is not to be distinguished absolutely from that in the first case. Whether the fruit which one eats has been found accidentally, or stolen or bought, makes not the slightest difference in the act of eating itself and in its direct consequences for the eater. Between desire and consumption lies the economic realm in unnumbered interrelationships. Now, economic activity appears to be an equalization of sacrifices and gains (of forces or objects), a mere form in the sense that it presupposes values as its content, in order to be able to draw them into the equalizing movement. But this appearance is not invincible. It will rather appear that the same process which constructs into an industrial system the values given as presuppositions itself produces the economic values.

To see this we need only remind ourselves in principle of the fact that the object is for us not a thing of value, so long as it is dissolved in the subjective process as an immediate stimulator of feelings, and thus at the same time is a self-evident competence of our sensibility. The object must first be detached from this sensibility, in order to acquire for our understanding the peculiar significance which we call value. For it is not only sure that desire, in and of itself, can never establish a value if it does not encounter obstacles. But if every desire could find its satisfaction without struggle and without diminution, an economic exchange of values would never come into existence. Indeed, desire itself would never have arisen to any considerable height if it could satisfy itself thus. It is only the postponement of the satisfaction through obstacles, the anxiety lest the object may escape, the tension of struggle for it, which brings into existence that aggregate of desire elements which may be designated as intensity or passion of volition.

If, however, even the highest energy of desire were generated wholly from within, yet we would not accord value to the object which satisfies the desire if it came to us in unlimited abundance. The important thing, in that case, would be the total enjoyment, the existence of which guarantees to us the satisfaction of our wishes, but not that particular quantum of which we actually take possession, because this could be replaced quite as easily by another. Our consciousness would in this case simply be filled with the rhythm of the subjective desires and satisfactions, without attaching any significance to the object mediating the satisfaction. The desire, therefore, which on its part came into existence only through an absence of feelings of satisfaction, a condition of want or limitation, is the psychological expression of the distance between the subject and the object which transmutes the subjective

This distance necessary to the consequence in question is produced in certain cases by exchange, sacrifice, abstinence from objects; that is, in a word, the foregoing of feelings of satisfaction. This takes place, now, in the form of traffic cotemporaneous between two actors, each of whom requires of the other the abstinence in question as condition of the feeling of satisfaction. The feeling of satisfaction, as must be repeatedly emphasized, would not place itself in antithesis with its object as a value in our consciousness if the value were always near to us, so that we should have no occasion to separate the object from that consequence in us which is alone interesting. Through exchange, that is, through the economic system, there arise at the same time the values of industry, because exchange is the vehicle or producer of the distance between the subject and the object which transmutes the subjective state of feeling into objective valuation. Kant once summarized his Theory of Knowledge in the proposition: "The conditions of experience are at the same time the conditions of the objects of experience." By this he meant that the process which we call experience and the conceptions which constitute its contents or objects are subject to the selfsame laws of the reason. The objects can come into our experience, that is, be experienced by us, because they are conceptions in us; and the same energy which makes and defines the experience has also manifested itself in the structure of the objects. In the same sense we may say here: The possibility of the economic system is, at the same time, the possibility of economic objects. The very procedure between two possessors of objects (substances, labor powers, rights, exchangeabilities of any sort), which procedure brings them into the so-called economic relationship, namely, reciprocal dedication, at the same time raises each of these objects into the category of values. The difficulty which threatens from the side of logic, namely, that the values must first exist, and exist as values, in order to enter into the form and movement of industry, is now obviated, by means of the perceived significance of the psychical relationship which we designated as the distance between us and the thing. This differentiates the original subjective state of feeling into, first, the desiring subject anticipating the feelings, and second, the object in antithesis with the subject, containing in itself the value; while the distance, on its side, is produced by exchange, that is, by the two-sided operation of limitations, restriction, abstinence. The *values* of industry emerge, therefore, in the same reciprocity and relativity in which the *economic character* of values consists.

This transference of the idea of economic value from the character of isolating substantiality into the living process of relation may be further explained on the ground of those factors which we are accustomed to regard as the constituents of value, namely, availability and rarity. Availability appears here as the first condition, based upon the constitution of the industrial actor, under which alone an object can under any circumstances come into question in economics. At the same time it is the presupposition of economic activity. In order that the value may reach a given degree, rarity must be associated with availability, as a characteristic of the objects themselves. If we wish to fix economic values through demand and supply, demand would correspond with availability, supply with rarity. For the availability would decide whether we demand the object at all, the rarity the price which we are compelled to pay. The availability serves as the absolute constituent of the economic—as that the extent of which must be determined in order that it may come into the course of economic exchange. We must from the beginning concede rarity as a merely relative element, since it means exclusively the quantitative relation in which the object in question stands to the existing aggregate of its kind; the qualitative nature of the object is not touched by its rarity. The availability, however, seems to exist before all economic action, all comparison, all relation with other objects, and as the substantial factor of economic activity, whose movements are dependent upon itself.

The circumstance whose efficacy is herewith outlined is not correctly designated by the notion of utility or serviceableness. What we mean in reality is the fact that the object is desired. All availability is, therefore, not in a situation to occasion economic operations with the object possessing the quality, if the availability does not at the same time have as a consequence that the objects are desired. As a matter of fact, this does not always occur. Any wish whatever may accord with any conception of things useful to us; actual desire, however, which has economic significance and which sets our acts in motion, is not present in such wishes, in case long poverty, constitutional laziness, diversion into other regions of interest, indifference of feeling toward the theoretically recognized utility, perceived impossibility of attaining the desired object, and other positive and negative elements work in the contrary direction. On the other hand, many sorts of things are desired by us, and also economically valued, which we cannot designate as useful or available without arbitrary distortion of verbal usage. Since, however, not everything that is available is also desired, if we decide to subsume everything that is economically desired under the concept of "availability," it is logically demanded that we shall make the fact of being desired the definitively decisive element for economic movement. Even with this correction the criterion is not absolute, totally separable from the relativity of valuation. In the first place, as we saw above, the desire itself does not come to conscious definiteness unless obstacles, difficulties, interpose themselves between the object and the subject. We do not desire actually until enjoyment of the object measures itself upon intermediaries, where at least the price of patience, of resignment of other exertion or enjoyment, places at a distance from us the object to conquer which is the essence of desire for it. Its economic value now, second, which rises upon the basis of its being desired, can consist only in heightening or sublimating of that relativity which resides in desire. For the desired object does not pass into practical value, that is, into value that enters into the industrial movement, until its desirability is compared with that of another object, and thereby acquires a measure. Only when a second object is present, with reference to which I am sure that I am willing to give it for the first object, or *vice versa*, has each of the two an assignable economic value. The mere desire for an object does not lead to this valuation, since it finds in itself alone no measure. Only the comparison of desires, that is, the exchangeability of their objects, fixes each of the same as a value defined in accordance with its scale, that is, an economic value. The intensity of the individual desire, in and of itself, need not have a cumulative effect upon the economic value of the object, for since the latter comes to expression only in exchange, desire can determine it only insofar as it modifies the exchange. If now I desire an object very intensely, its exchange value is not thereby determined, for either I have the object *not yet* in my possession (in which case my desire, if I do not manifest it, can exert no influence upon the demand of the present possessor; he will rather adjust his claims according to the measure of his own interest in the object, or in accordance with his suppositions with reference to average interest), or, I *have* the object in my possession (in which case my terms will be either so high that the object is entirely excluded from exchange, in which instance it is to that extent no longer an economic value, or my demands must fall to the measure of the interest which a calculating person takes in the object). The decisive factor is this: That the economic, practically effective value is never a value in the abstract, but rather in its essence and idea a determined quantum of value; that this quantity in general can come into existence only through measurements of two intensities of desire against each other; that the form in which this measurement takes place within the industrial system is that of reciprocal gain and sacrifice; that consequently the economic object does not, as superficially appears, possess in its desirability an absolute element of value, but rather that this fact of being desired operates to give the object a value exclusively as being the foundation or the material of an actual or putative exchange.

Even in case we derive the valuation of objects from an absolute motive, namely, the labor expended upon them, and even if we assert that the value of goods is in inverse ratio to the productive capacity of the labor, yet we must still recognize the determination of the value of the objects as purely reciprocal, instead of a derivative from a single absolute standard. This being admitted, there arises the following relationship: A pair of boots has at a given time the same value as twenty meters of shirting. If now, through a new arrangement, the total labor demanded for the boots falls to one-half, they are worth only ten meters of shirting. Suppose now the labor time demanded for shirting is reduced one-half by improved machinery; the boots will then once more be the equivalent to twenty meters of shirting. If, again, the corresponding improvement affects all the laborers, and no goods are introduced which affect the relations between them, the two articles remain unchanged in their value as expressed in terms of each other. The change in the productive power of labor has an influence upon the value of the products only when it affects *isolated portions* of the economic organism, but not when it affects the organism as a whole. However we may exert ourselves, therefore, to express the value of the object through an absolute quantitative symbol, however qualified, it remains still only the *relation*, in which the various wares participate in this vehicle of value, which determines the value of each. Even under that presupposition, it is for the value of the separate objects as individuals wholly irrelevant how much or how little labor is invested in them. Only insofar as it is a quantity of labor greater or less in comparison with the quantity of labor invested in another object does each of the two acquire an economically effective value. But for the same reason it is, on the other hand, also unwarranted to complain at absence of the necessary stability of value in the daily wage of labor—by which expression it is implied that the average return of a day's labor is a value-unity. That accusation is founded on the fact that the labor day constantly increases in productivity and power in exchange. Assuming, however, for the moment that labor is the one creator of value, the value of the time-unit of labor *for the purpose of exchange of related goods* is always the same; although, absolutely considered, it has increased, and corresponds to a larger quantum of each separate product. Since the reciprocal relation of the goods has remained the same, the relation of the labor time to each is the same as to the others. It may, therefore, remain, for the purpose of reckoning their relative values, a constant term.

This relativity of value, in consequence of which the given things stimulating feeling and desire come to be values only in the reciprocity of the give-and-take process, *appears* to lead to the consequence that value is nothing but the price, and that between the two objects no differences of scale can exist. Consequently, the frequent falling away of the two from each other would refute the theory. Against that undeniable fact of varying ratio our theory asserts, to be sure, that there would never have been such a thing as a value if the universal phenomenon which we call price had not emerged. That a thing is worth something in a purely economic sense means that it is worth *something* to me, that is, that I am ready to give something for it. What in the world can move us to go beyond that naive subjective enjoyment of the things themselves, and to credit to them that peculiar significance which we call their value? This certainly cannot come from their scarcity in and of itself, for if this existed simply as a fact, and were not in some way or other modifiable by us, we would regard it as a natural, and, on account of the defective differentiations, a perhaps entirely unrecognized quality of the external cosmos. For, since it could not be otherwise, it would receive no emphasis beyond its inherent qualities. This valuation arises only from the fact that something must be paid for things: the patience of waiting, the effort of search, the application of labor power, the abstinence from things otherwise desirable. Without price, therefore—price originally in this extensive sense—value does not come into being. That of two objects the one is more valuable than the other comes to pass subjectively as well as objectively only where one agent is ready to give this for that, but conversely that is not to be obtained for this. In transactions that have not become complicated the higher or lower value can be only the consequence or the expression of this immediate practical will to exchange. And if we say we exchange the things for each other because they are equally valuable, it is only that frequent inversion of thought and speech by which we also say that things pleased us because they were beautiful, whereas, in reality, they are beautiful because they please us.

If, thus, value is at the same time the offspring of price, it seems to be an identical proposition that their height must be the same. I refer now to the above proof, that in each individual case no contracting party pays the price which is to him, under the given circumstances, too high for the thing obtained. If in the poem of Chamisso the highwayman at the point of the pistol compels the victim to sell him his watch and rings for three coppers, the fact is that under the circumstances, since the victim could not otherwise save his life, the thing obtained in exchange was actually worth the price. No laborer would work for starvation wages if, in the situation in which he actually found himself, he did not prefer this wage to not working. The appearance of paradox in the assertion of the equivalence of value and price in every individual case arises only from the fact that certain conceptions of *other kinds* of equivalence of value and price are brought into our estimate of the case. The relative stability of the relationships by which the majority of exchanges are determined, on the other hand the analogies which fix still uncertain value relations according to the norm of others already existing, produce the conceptions: if for a definite object this and that other definite object were exchange equivalents, these two or this group of objects would have equality in the scale of value, and if abnormal circumstances caused us to exchange the one object for values higher or lower in the scale, price and value would fall away from each other, although in each individual case, as a matter of fact, under consideration of *its* circumstances, they would coincide. We should not forget that the objective and just equivalence of value and price which we make the norm of the actual and the specific works only under very definite historical and technical conditions; and, with change of these conditions, at once vanishes. Between the norm itself and the cases which are characterized as exceptional or as adequate, no general difference exists, but, so to speak, only a numerical difference—somewhat as we say of an extraordinarily eminent or degraded individual, "He is really no longer a man." The fact is that this idea of man is only an average; it would lose its normative character at the moment in which the majority of men ascended or descended to that grade, which then would pass for the generically human.

In order to reach this perception we must, to be sure, extricate ourselves from deep-rooted conceptions of value, which also have an assured practical justification. These conceptions, in the case of relationships that are somewhat complex, rest in two strata with reference to each other. The one is formed from the traditions of society, from the majority of experiences, from demands that seem to be purely logical; the other, from individual correlations, from the demands of the moment, from the constraint of given facts. In contrast with the rapid changes within this latter stratum, the gradual evolution of the former and its construction out of elaboration of our perceptions is lost to sight, and the former appears as alone justified *as the expression of an objective ratio.* Where now, in case of an exchange under the given circumstances, the valuations of sacrifice and gain at least balance each other—for otherwise no agent would consummate the exchange—yet judged by those general criteria a discrepancy appears, in such a case we speak of a divergence between value and price. This occurs most decisively under the two presuppositions (almost always united), viz., first, that a single value quality passes as economic value in general, and two objects consequently can be recognized as equal in value, only in so far as the like quantum of that fundamental value is present in them; and, second, that a definite proportion between two values appears as a something that must be, with the emphasis of a not merely objective, but also a moral demand. The conception, for example, that the essential value element in all values is the labor time objectified in them is utilized in both these assumptions, and thus gives a direct or an indirect standard which fixes the value independent of price, and makes the latter vibrate in changing plus and minus differences, as compared with the former. Now it is evident, to be sure, that if we from the start recognize only a single value substance, only that price corresponds to the value so contained which contains precisely an equivalent amount of that same value. According to this principle the values should be the first and fixed element; the price should constitute a more or less adequate secondary element. But this consequence, supposing everything else is conceded, does not in fact follow. The fact of that single *measure* of value leaves entirely unexplained how labor power comes to have value. It would hardly have occurred if the labor power had not, by acting upon various materials and by creating various products, made the possibility of exchange; or unless the exercise of the power had been recognized as a sacrifice made for the gain of the object achieved by the sacrifice. Thus labor power also comes into the value category through the possibility and reality of exchange, quite unaffected by the circumstance that later labor power may itself furnish a measure, *within* the value category, for the other contents. If the labor power is thus also the content of that value, it receives its form as value only through the fact that it enters into the relation of sacrifice and gain, or price and value (here in the narrower sense). In the cases of discrepancy between price and value, the one contracting party would, according to this theory, give a quantum of immediately realizable labor power for a lesser quantum of the same. Yet other circumstances, not containing labor power, are in such wise connected with this case that the party still completes the exchange; for example: the satisfaction of an economic need, amateurish fancy, fraud, monopoly, and similar circumstances. In the wider and subjective sense, therefore, the equivalence of value and counter-value remains in these cases, while the simple norm, labor power, which makes the discrepancy possible, does not on its side cease to derive its genesis as a vehicle of value from exchange.

The qualitative determination of objects, which subjectively signifies their desirability, can consequently not maintain the claim of constituting an absolute value magnitude. It is always the relation of the desires to each other, realized in exchange, which makes their objects economic values. This determination appears more immediately in connection with the other element supposed to constitute value, namely, scarcity, or relative rarity. Exchange is, indeed, nothing else than the inter-individual attempt to improve conditions rising out of scarcity of goods; that is, to reduce as far as possible the amount of subjective abstinence by the mode of distributing the given stock. Thereupon follows immediately a universal correlation between that which we call *scarcity value* and that which we call *exchange value*, a correlation which appears, for instance, in the relation of socialism to both. We may, perhaps, indicate the economic purposes of socialism comprehensively and abstractly in this way, namely, that it strives to abolish scarcity value; that is, that modification of the value of things which arises from their rarity or abundance; for it is abundance which reduces the value of labor. There should be less labor, in order that labor may be appraised according to the quality value, without depression on account of the quantity. On the other hand, the means of enjoyment should lose that value which they now have on account of their restricted quantity; that is, they should be accessible to all. Accordingly, Marx held that in the capitalistic type of society, that is, the sort of society which socialism wishes to abolish, exchange value alone is decisive, while use value no longer plays any rôle. While socialism despises exchange value quite as much as scarcity value, it calls attention to the radical connection between the two.

For us, however, the connection is more important in the reverse direction. I have already emphasized the fact that scarcity of goods would scarcely have a valuation of them as a consequence if it were not modifiable by us. It is, however, modifiable in two ways: either through devotion of labor power, which increases the stock of the goods in question, or through devotion of already possessed objects, which as substitutes abolish the rarity of the most desired objects for the individual. Accordingly, we may say immediately that the scarcity of goods in proportion to the desires centering upon them objectively determines exchange; that, however, the exchange on its side brings scarcity into force as an element of value. It is a thoroughgoing mistake of theories of value to assume that, when utility and rarity are given, economic value—that is, exchange movement—is something to be taken for granted, a conceptually necessary consequence of those premises. In this they are by no means correct. In case, for instance, there were alongside of these presuppositions an ascetic renunciation, or if they only instigated to conflict or robbery—which is, to be sure, often enough the case—no economic value and no economic life would emerge. Exchange is a sociological structure *sui generis*, a primary form and function of inter-individual life, which by no means emerges as a logical consequence from those qualitative and quantitative properties of things which we call availability and rarity. On the contrary, it is rather the case that these two properties derive their value-creating significance only under the presupposition of exchange. Where exchange, the offering of a sacrifice for the purpose of a gain, is for any reason excluded, there no rarity of the desired object can confer upon it economic value until the possibility of that relation reappears. We may express the relation in this way: The significance of the object for the individual always rests merely in its desirability; so far as that is concerned which the object is to do for us, its qualitative character is decisive, and when we have it, it is a matter of indifference in this respect whether there exist besides many, few, or no specimens of the same sort. (I do not treat here especially the cases in which rarity itself is a species of qualitative character, which makes the object desirable to us, as in the case of old postage stamps, curiosities, antiquities without æsthetic or historical value, etc. I also disregard other cases, interesting in themselves, here however in principle insignificant, namely, those psychological subsidiary phenomena which frequently arise from scarcity itself, where they have no effect upon acquisition of the object.) The enjoyment of things, therefore, so soon as possession of them is achieved, the positive practical significance of their actuality for us, is quite independent of the scarcity question, since this affects only a numerical relation to things, which we do not have, to be sure, but which, according to the hypothesis, we do not desire to have. The only question in point with reference to things, apart from enjoyment of them, is the way to them. So soon as this way is a long and difficult one, leading over sacrifice in the shape of strain of the patience, disappointment, labor, self-denial, etc., we call the object scarce. Paradoxical as it is, things are not difficult to obtain because they are scarce, but they are scarce because they are difficult to obtain. The inflexible external fact that there is a deficient stock of certain goods to satisfy all our desires for them would be in itself insignificant. Whether they are scarce in the sense of economic value is decided simply by the circumstance of the measure of energy, patience, devotion to acquisition, which is necessary in order to obtain them. Let us suppose a stock of goods which suffices to cover all the demands centered upon it, but which is so disposed that every portion of it is to be obtained only with considerable effort and sacrifice. Then the result for its valuation and its practical significance would be precisely the same which, under the presupposition of equal availability, we have been accustomed to derive from its scarcity. The difficulty of attainment, that is, the magnitude of the sacrifice involved in exchange, is thus the element that peculiarly constitutes value. Scarcity constitutes only the external appearance of this element, only the externalizing of it in the form of quantity. We fail to observe that scarcity, purely as such, is only a negative property, an existence characterized by a non-existence. The non-existent, however, cannot be operative. Every positive consequence must proceed from a positive property and force, of which that negative property is only the shadow. These concrete energies are, however, manifestly only those that are put into action in the exchange, so that the increase of value starts from that increasing magnitude whose negative is the scarcity of the object.

Finally, by way of corollary, I will add a more conceptual deduction, namely, that the usual conception of the scarcity theory must presuppose the value which it tries to derive from scarcity. According to this conception, an object of economic desire acquires value if no unlimited number of specimens of its kind is at hand; that is, if the present quantity of such objects does not cover a series of needs that look to it for satisfaction. The failure of these needs to be covered is felt as a painful condition which ought not to be, as the negation of value. The covering of these needs must be something having value. Otherwise the failure could exert no such effect. If, however, this defect is necessary to establish the value of the present quantity, the value is thereby presupposed whose establishment is in question. The existing quantity has value because the lacking quantity has value. Otherwise its lack could never establish a value. Let us suppose the quantity A, which would completely cover the need, to be divided into two parts: first, the portion actually present, M, and, second, the merely ideally present, N. According to the theory, the value M is determined by the fact that N is not present. N must, as we said, have a value in order to produce this consequence. In order that it may have this value, we must, however, think it as present, and, on the contrary, M as not present. Otherwise the whole of A would be accessible, and therefore, according to the scarcity theory, no portion of it would have a value. The value of the actual quantity is based on that of the non-existing quantity, that of the non-existing quantity (which I must think in this connection as present) on that of the existing quantity (which I must consider non-existent). The scarcity element is thus to be accounted for only relatively, equally with that element which has its source in the

66

significance of the object for the feelings. As little as the fact of being desired can scarcity create for the object a valuation otherwise than in the reciprocal relation with another object existing under like conditions. We may examine the one object ever so closely with reference to its self-sufficient properties, we shall never find the economic value; since this consists exclusively in the *reciprocal relationship*, which comes into being between several objects on the basis of these properties, each determining the other, and each giving to the other the significance which each in turn receives from the other.

4

Sociological Aesthetics*

THE OBSERVATION OF HUMAN ACTIONS owes its continuously renewed challenge to the infinitely varied mixture between the steady return of a few basic elements and the fullness of their individual variations. The trends, developments and contrasts of human history can be reduced to a surprisingly small number of original themes. What has been said about poetry—that lyric and dramatic writing consists in changing formulations of a narrowly limited number of possibilities of fate—is valid for every other area of human activity. The more broadly we conceptualize these areas, the smaller becomes the number of basic themes. Finally, when life is viewed in the most general way, they will almost always end in a dialetic whose struggles, compromises or combinations, generate all the continuously novel forms of life. Every epoch of human history seems to derive its unlimited number of manifestations from this dualism between movements of thought and life, in which the basic streams of humanity find their most simple expression. This deep, living antithesis in human affairs can be conceptualized only through symbols and examples. During each major historical period a different shape of this contrast appears as its basic type and original form.

Thus, in the beginning of Greek philosophy there appeared the important contrast between Heraclitus and the Eleatic School. To Heraclitus, all being was in continuous flux; the processes of this world were given form in the variety of unlimited contrasts which continuously transformed themselves from one into the other. For the Eleatic School, however, there was only a single static essence which transcended

* A translation of "Soziologische Aesthetik," *Die Zukunft*, 17 (1896) 204–216.

the deceiving appearance of the senses. It was all inclusive and undivided, and it incorporated the absolute undifferentiated unity of all things. This was the basic form which the division of all human essence took in Greek thought, and provided the theme for its whole development. With Christianity there appeared a different elaboration: the contrast between the sacred and the secular principles. For all specifically Christian life, this appeared as a final and absolute antithesis between essential orientations, from which all differences between willing and thinking had to be derived. By itself, however, it did not lead to any deeper distinction. More recent perspectives of life developed these elements into the fundamental contrasts between nature and spirit. Finally, the present has found for this dualism the formulae of social versus individual, which draws its line through mankind and even through the individual man. A typical difference between the characters of men and institutions appears to be expressed by this dichotomy as if it were a watershed from which they separate in different directions only to flow together again and influence reality according to their degree of participation. The line seems to extend through all questions of life, to the most remote concerns; it appears in the most varied subjects. In socio-political life it is expressed by the contrast between socialistic and individualistic tendencies. It determines not only the depths of purely materialistic interest in life, but also the heights of aesthetic value.

The essence of aesthetic contemplation and interpretation for us consists in the following: What is unique emphasizes what is typical, what is accidental appears as normal, and the superficial and fleeting stands for what is essential and basic. It seems to be impossible for any phenomenon to avoid being reduced to what is important and of eternal value. Even the lowest, intrinsically ugly phenomenon can be dissolved into contexts of color and form, of feeling and experience, which provide it with exciting significance. To involve ourselves deeply and lovingly with the even most common product, which, would be banal and repulsive in its isolated appearance, enables us to conceive of it, too, as a ray and image of the final unity of all things from which beauty and meaning flow. Every philosophical system, every religion, every moment of our heightened emotional experience searches for symbols which are appropriate for their expression. If we pursue this possibility of aesthetic appreciation to its final point, we find that there are no essential differences among things. Our world view turns into aesthetic pantheism. Every point contains within itself the potential of being redeemed to absolute aesthetic importance. To the adequately trained eye the totality of beauty, the complete meaning of the world as a whole, radiates from every single point.

Thereby, however, the individual object loses the significance which it possesses precisely as an individual and in contrast with everything else. For it is impossible to conserve individuality by saying that aesthetic formulations and the deepening of the things are equally possible everywhere and provide full freedom for the expression of different qualities and contents of beauty. Nor can it be preserved by saying that there exists only aesthetic comparability and not equality of value, or that only differences of rank were cancelled out in this area but not the colors and color values, the meanings and thoughts, or the allegro and adagio. This conception, which wishes to reconcile the stimuli of universal aesthetic equivalence (*Allgleichheit*) and uniqueness (*Alleinheit*) with those of aesthetic individualism, does not fully satisfy the demands of the latter. The hierarchy of values, the rise of the significant over the run-of-the-mill product, the organic growth and development which permit the molding of the inspired out of the dull and the refined out of the raw, provide a background, height and power of light, which, under conditions of equal aesthetic value of objects could not be reached by any other one among them. From them comes forth an equally sublime radiance over all things which raises the lowest to that of the highest but also brings the highest to equal rank with the lowest.

Our sensations are tied to differences, those of value no less than the sensations of touch or temperature. We are not always able to proceed at a constant level, at least not on the highest level which is accessible to us during our best moments. Therefore we have to pay for raising the lowest level to aesthetic heights by denying ourselves those upswings which can occur only rarely and sporadically, and can rise only above the level of a lower undifferentiated and darker world. It is not only this conditioning of all our sensations by differences, which we may conceive of as undesirable restraints and shortcomings of our being, that ties the values of things to their relative distances from one another: these very distances, too, represent bases of aesthetic value. One of the highest aesthetic stimuli and values of this world is based on the division of the world into light and darkness, so that its elements do not flow into one another formlessly, but instead each individual has its place in a hierarchy of values between a higher and lower one, and the raw and lower forms derive their existential meaning from their being the support and background for the refined, bright, and exalted. Thus, irreconcilable approaches are divided. One finds rewards in a thousand undistinguished abysses for the sake of one height, and deduces the value of things from this highest perfection which reflects the value and meaning of all lower things. Someone who values things this way will never understand another who hears the voice of God in a worm and feels complete justice in the claim of each thing to be valued equally with any other. Moreover, he who does not wish to deny himself the drama of structuring, grading, and forming the world's image according to the amount of its beauty, will never be able to share the world intimately with another person who sees the harmony of things in their equality, so that charm and ugliness of appearance, ridiculous chaos and meaningful form, represent only covering veils behind which he will always see identical beauty and the soul of being for which his mind thirsts.

If we were to search for a reconciliation here, for a conceptual perspective which could demonstrate these value schemes to be compatible and resolved on a higher level on the ground that both, even though under divided jurisdictions, rule many individuals—this would indeed be like trying to prove that there is no contrast between day and night because of the existence of dusk. Here we stand at the springs of all human life. Depending on the areas of human experience through which they flow, they will nourish the immense contrasts between political socialism and individualism, or pantheistic and atomistic forms of knowledge, or aesthetic equalization and differentiation. These sources themselves, these final bases of essence, cannot be described adequately with words. They can only be recognized in those individual phenomena in which they are mixed. If they cannot be conceptualized, at least one can point them out as those unknown forces which give form to the matter of our existence. They are never reconciled, yet each provides to the other fresh stimulation, which gives the life of our species its restlessness, struggle, and vacillation between contrasts, so that the appeasement of either one calls forth the strongest stimulation for the other. In this process only lies what we might call their reconciliation: not in the dull proof by which they might be conceptually reduced to unity, but in the demonstration that they continuously confront and even fight one another within a single species of being, even in each single soul. This is precisely the height and grandeur of the human soul: its very liveliness, its ungrasped unity, permit during each moment the expression of forces which flow from completely irreconcilable sources towards completely different goals.

The origin of all aesthetic themes is found in symmetry. Before man can bring an idea, meaning, harmony into things, he must first form them symmetrically. The various parts of the whole must be balanced against one another, and arranged evenly around a center. In this fashion man's form-giving power, in contrast to the contingent and confused character of mere nature, becomes most quickly, visibly, and immediately clear. Thus, the first aesthetic step leads beyond a mere acceptance of the meaninglessness of things to a will to transform them symmetrically. As aesthetic values are refined and deepened, however, man returns to the irregular and asymmetrical. It is in symmetrical formations that rationalism first emerges. So long as life is still instinctive, affective and irrational, aesthetic redemption from it takes on such a rationalistic form. Once intelligence, reckoning, balance have penetrated it, the aesthetic need once again changes into its opposite, seeking the irrational and its external form, the asymmetrical.

The lower level of the aesthetic drive finds expression in the building of systems which arrange objects into symmetric pictures. Thus, for example, the penance-books of the sixth century arranged sins and punishments in systems of mathematical precision and balanced structure. Hence the first attempt to master intellectually the totality of moral errors was cast in the form of a scheme which was as mechanical, rational, and symmetric as possible. Once these errors were brought under the yoke of the system, the mind could grasp them the most quickly and with the least resistance. The system breaks down as soon as man has intellectually mastered the proper meaning of the object and need no longer derive it only from its relations with others; at this point, therefore, there is a weakening of the aesthetic will to symmetry, with which the elements were previously arranged.

It is possible to discover through an analysis of the role of symmetry in social life how apparently purely aesthetic interests are called forth by materialistic purposes, and how, on the other hand, aesthetic motives affect forms which seem to obey only functional purposes. For example, in a variety of older cultures we find the coordination of ten members of groups into special social units—for military, taxable, juridical, and other purposes—which in turn frequently form a higher unit, the hundred, by the combination of ten such groups. The reason for this symmetrical construction of groups was certainly the advantage of easier survey, demarcation, and control. The peculiarly stylized society which grew from this type of organization developed on account of its mere utility. But the meaning of "the hundred" extended beyond its utility. Thus "hundreds" frequently contained more or less than one hundred individuals. During the Middle Ages, for example, the Senate of Barcelona was called the "one hundred" even though it numbered approximately two hundred members. This deviation from the original organizational rationality demonstrates a transition from use value to aesthetic value, to the charm of symmetry and architectural forms in social life, while the fiction of technical rationality is still being maintained.

This tendency to organize all of society symmetrically and equally structured according to general principles is shared by all despotic forms of social organization. Justus Moeser wrote in 1772:

> The gentlemen of the Central Administrative Department would like to reduce everything to simple rules. In this fashion we remove ourselves from the true plan of nature, which shows its wealth in variety, and we clear the way for despotism, which will coerces everything under a few rules.

Symmetrical organizations facilitate the ruling of many from a single point. Norms can be imposed from above with less resistance and greater effectiveness in a symmetrical organization than in a system whose inner structure is irregular and fluctuating. For this reason Charles V (1519–1556) intended to level out all unequal and peculiar political structures and privileges in the Netherlands and to restructure them into an organization which would be comparable in all parts. A historian of the epoch writes "that he hated the old licenses and stubborn privileges, which disturbed his ideas of symmetry." Egyptian pyramids have correctly been designated as symbols of the political organization of great Oriental despots. They represent the completely symmetrical structure of a society whose elements in the upward direction rapidly decline in number while their amounts of power increase until they meet in the pinnacle which rules equally over the whole.

Even though this form of organization derived its rationality from the needs of despotism, it generates a formal, purely aesthetic meaning. This charm of symmetry, with its internal equilibration, its external unity, and its harmonic relationship of all parts to its unified center, is one of the purely aesthetic forces which attracts many intelligent people to autocracy, with its unlimited expression of the unified will of the State. This is why genuinely liberal forms of the state tend towards asymmetry. Macaulay, the inspired liberal, points directly to this feature as the proper strength of British constitutional life.

> We do not think about its symmetry but a great deal about its utility. We never remove an anomaly only because it is an anomaly. We never set our norms for a wider area than is demanded by the special case with which we are dealing at the moment. These are the rules which taken as a whole have goverened the proceedings of our 250 parliaments from King John to Queen Victoria.

Here the ideal of symmetry and logical closure, which gives meaning to everything from one single point, is rejected in favor of another ideal, which permits each element to develop independently according to its own conditions. The whole, of course, thus looks disorganized and irregular. Nevertheless, in addition to all concrete motives, there is an aesthetic charm even in this lack of symmetry, in this liberation of the individual. This overtone can easily be heard in the words of

Macaulay. It derives from the feeling that this form of organization brings the inner life of the state, to its most typical expression and its most harmonic form.

The influence of aesthetic forces upon social facts is most vivid in modern conflicts between socialistic and individualistic tendencies. Without any doubt, certain ideas of socialism are based on aesthetic values. That society as a whole should become a work of art in which every single element attains its meaning by virtue of its contribution to the whole; that a unified plan should rationally determine all of production, instead of the present rhapsodic haphazardness by which the efforts of individuals benefit or harm society; that the wasteful competition and the fight of individuals against individuals should be replaced by the absolute harmony of work—all these ideas of socialism no doubt meet aesthetic interests. Whatever else one may have against it, these ideas at any rate refute the popular opinion that socialism both begins and ends exclusively in the needs of the stomach. The social question therefore is not only an ethical question, but also an aesthetic one.[1]

Quite apart from its consequences for the individual, the rational organization of society has a high aesthetic attraction. It aims to make the totality of lives in the whole organization into a work of art, which at present can hardly be accomplished for the life of an individual. The more we learn to appreciate composite forms, the more readily we will extend aesthetic categories to forms of society as a whole. Consider, for example, the aesthetic appeal of machines: the absolute purposiveness and reliability of motions, the extreme reduction of resistance and friction, the harmonic integration of the most minute and the largest parts, provides machines with a peculiar beauty. The organization of a factory and the plan of the socialistic state only repeats this beauty on larger scales. This peculiar interest in harmony and symmetry by which socialism demonstrates its rationalistic character, and by which it aims to stylize social life, is expressed purely externally by the fact that socialistic utopias are always set up according to principles of symmetry. Towns or buildings are arranged either in circular or quadratic form. The layout of the capital is mathematically constructed in the Sun-State of Campanella, as are the work assignments for the citizens and the gradations of their rights and duties. This general trait of socialistic plans attests to the deep power of attraction in the idea of an harmonic, internally balanced organization of human activity overcoming all resistance of irrational individuality. This interest, a purely aesthetic one, independent of all material consequences, has probably always been important in determining the social forms of life.

The attractiveness of beauty is sometimes described as a saving of

74

thought, an unravelling of a maximum number of images with minimum effort. If this is so, then the symmetrical construction of social groups, as it is desired by socialism, will fulfill these postulates. On the other hand, an individuated society, characterized by heterogeneous interests and irreconcilable tendencies, embracing many series of development which have been commenced and interrupted innumerable times (since they were only carried on by individuals), presents to the mind a restless, uneven image, which continuously requires new nervous exertion and effort for its understanding. But a socialistic and balanced society through its organic unity, its symmetrical arrangement and mutual coordination of movements in common centers, provides for the observing mind a maximum of insight. To understand the social picture here requires a minimum of intellectual effort. This fact in its aesthetic significance would seem to figure decisively in the intellectual appeal of socialism.

In aesthetics, symmetry means the dependence of individual elements on their mutual interdependence with all others, but also self-containment within the designated circle. Asymmetrical arrangements permit broader individual rights, more latitude for the free and far-reaching relations of each element. The internal organization of socialism takes this into consideration; thus it is no accident that all historical approximations to socialism occurred only within strictly closed groups which declined all relations to outside powers. This containment, which is appropriate for the aesthetic character of symmetry as well as for the political character of the socialistic state, suggests the general argument that because of continuous international intercourse socialism could never come to power in a single country but only uniformly in the whole civilized world.

The power of aesthetic valuation is demonstrated by the fact that it can also be applied equally well in support of the opposite social ideal. Beauty, as it is actually felt today, has an almost exclusively individualistic character. Essentially it is based on individual traits, in contrast to the general characteristics and conditions of life. Truly romantic beauty is based to a large extent on the opposition and isolation of the individual from what is common and valid for everybody. This is true even if we disavow individualism on ethical grounds. It is aesthetically attractive to think of the individual not only as a member of a larger whole, but as a whole in its own right, which as such no longer fits into any symmetric organization. Even the most perfect social mechanism is only a mechanism, and so lacks the freedom which, regardless of one's philosophical interpretations, is the *sine qua non* of beauty. Thus, of the world-views which have become prominent during recent times, those of Rembrandt and Nietzsche are most decidedly individualistic, and are supported by distinctly aesthetic motives. Indeed, the individualism of this contemporary view of beauty extends so far that even flowers, and especially modern garden flowers, are no longer bound into bundles. On the contrary, they are arranged individually, or several of them at most are bound together rather loosely. Thus every single garden flower is seen as an individual in itself; they are all aesthetic individualities, which cannot be coordinated into symmetrical unity. By contrast, wild flowers, which are less developed and somehow arrested in their evolution, form delightful bunches.

This combination of similar stimuli with irreconcilable contrasts points to the peculiar origin of aesthetic feelings. Even though we know very little about it with certainty, we sense that the utility of objects for the preservation and enhancement of the species also forms the starting point for their aesthetic value. Perhaps something appears to us as beautiful which the species has found useful; perhaps it provides us with enjoyment because we are part of the species, even though as individuals we no longer enjoy the real utility of the object. This immediate utility has been cleared away in the course of historical development and inheritance; the materialistic motives on which our aesthetic sensibilities are based have been effaced in time. Hence they gave to beauty the character of "pure form," and a certain other-worldliness and non-reality not unlike the purifying spirit which hovers over one's own experiences of past times.

Utility, however, can take many forms. What is useful may frequently be of sharply contrasting content during various adaptive periods, or in different regions during the same period of time. Major alternatives of historical life gain prominence through widely varying historical conditions. For social organization, for example, the individual is only a member and an element. Likewise, from the perspective of individuals, society is only a base point. At any given moment these emphases are mixed in changing proportions. On this basis the pre-conditions are given towards which the aesthetic interests of a certain social form of life may turn as strongly towards one or another. We are led to an apparent contradiction: the aesthetic charm of a totality in which the individual disappears seems to grow with the prominence on the individual. But this can be resolved without further ado, if we see all feeling for beauty as the distillation, the idealization, the mature form of the adaptations and feelings of utility of the species in an individual member, who has inherited its consciousness, but in a spiritualized and formalistic way. The great variety and contradiction of historical developments are thus reflected in the breadth of our aesthetic sensitivity. Hence we can connect an equally strong stimulus to the most opposite poles of social interest.

The intrinsic significance of artistic styles can be interpreted as a result of different distances which they produce between us and phenomena. All art forms change the field of vision by which we originally and naturally react to reality. On the one hand, art brings us closer to reality, bringing us into a more immediate relationship with its proper and innermost meaning by revealing to us behind the cold strangeness of the world the animated quality of being (*Sein*) through which it becomes familiar and intelligible for us. On the other hand, every artistic medium introduces abstractions from the immediacy of material things. It weakens concrete stimuli and introduces a veil between them and us, analogous to the blue hue which surrounds distant mountains. Equally strong stimuli are connected with both ends of this antithesis. Tensions and different emphases between them express in each style its unique form. In "naturalistic" art, in its opposition to all proper "stylization," closeness to the natural object seems to be dominant. Naturalistic art intends to find in each little element of this world its inner significance. Formalistic art, on the contrary, places between us and the objects a preconceived postulate concerning beauty and significance.

All art forms are nourished by immediate impressions of reality, even though they become art only when they grow beyond this level. In order to convince us of its truth and importance, art demands an unconscious process of reduction. This reduction is short and easy in naturalistic art forms. For this reason naturalistic art does not require determined and far-reaching intellectual activities for its enjoyment; its approaches are quite direct. Thus there may often be a relationship between naturalistic art and sensual lust, though this is not at all necessary. In any case, man can be most quickly and most directly excited by naturalistic art, because the object and the subjective reactions to it are here in closest proximity.

Nevertheless, naturalism uses the refined charm of remote effects. We note the careful search for its objects and motives in the daily life, in undeveloped forms and in banal expressions. For a very sensitive beholder, the peculiar distance between works of art and the immediacy of experience becomes especially clear when the object is very close. For less delicate perception, a greater distance from the object itself is required for the enjoyment of this charm of distance, as for example in stylized Italian landscapes or paintings of historical dramas. The less cultivated (and childlike) aesthetic feelings are, the more fantastic, the farther removed from reality the object must be by which the artistic work achieves its impact. A more sensitive viewer does not require such a materialistic prop. The artistic form of the object in itself provides him with secret charm of distance from things, liberates him from their dull pressure, carries him from the realm of nature to that of spirit. He will experience this even more intensely when art deals with proximate, low and relatively secular material.

It is interesting that contemporary aesthetics strongly emphasizes the distance between subject and object, rather than the intimacy. This special interest in items from a distance seems to be a distinctive sign of modern times, which is common to many phenomena. The preference for cultures and styles removed in space and time belongs here. Things from a distance best stimulate many vividly changing imaginations, and thus fulfill our multifarious need for excitement. But these strange and distant things have relatively weak effects on our imagination, because they have no direct relationship to our personal interests. Thus they impose on our weakened nerves only comfortable excitement. This is the impact of all the fragments, suggestions, aphorisms, symbols, and primitive art forms which are evoking such vivid responses now. All of these forms of expression, which are at home in all the arts, separate us from the completeness and fullness of the things themselves. They speak to us as if they were at a distance. They represent reality not with direct certainty, but with a kind of retracted acuity. The literary style of the late nineteenth century, most fully developed in Paris and Vienna, avoids the direct designation of things, describes only minor points and covers verbally only one of the sides; here mode of expression and subject matter coincide only in the most isolated details. The pathological symptom of *Beruhrungsangst*, the fear of getting into too close contact with objects, is spread endemically in a mild degree nowadays. It grows out of a kind of hyperaesthetics, for which every live and immediate contact produces pain. For this reason the aestheticism of the majority of modern men is expressed through negative taste. Illustrations are: the easy vulnerability to disagreeable items, the determined exclusion of the unpleasant, the repulsion of many if not most varieties of stimuli. On the other hand, lack of balance comes about from expressing positive taste, from energetically saying "yes," from the happy and unrestrained acceptance of what is liked, in short, from all actively appropriating energies.

Naturalism in its cruder forms was a desperate attempt to overcome distance, to catch the closeness and immediacy of things. But as soon as men got close, their sensitive nerves were unable even to tolerate the contact, and they shied away as if they had touched hot coals. This happened not only in painting, as represented by the Scottish school, or literature, which turned from *Zolaism* to symbolism; it happened in science as well. For example, materialism, which seeks to grasp reality immediately, has been swamped by neo-Kantian or subjectivistic worldviews, according to which things must be broken down or distilled through the medium of the soul before they become true knowledge. Again, in all scientific disciplines, a call has risen for coordination and generalization which can attain a distance capable of viewing all concrete individual facts. In ethics, too, concrete utility has to step behind more abstract, "spiritualized" principles, which are frequently religious and always far from sensual immediacy.

The tendency of our culture towards distance is observable in more than one dominant way. (I am using the quantitative dimension of distance only as a symbol, an approximation, since there is no other more direct expression for what is going on.) The dissolution of the family is connected with this development. So is the feeling of unbearable narrowness which is frequently awakened in modern man by his circle of close relatives, which frequently involves him in very tragic forms of conflict. This fear of contact is reinforced by the ease of travel over longer distances. The wealth of intimate relations which are now possible with spatially and temporarily remote parties seems to make us more and more sensitive to the shocks and disturbances which come to us from the immediate proximity and contact between man and things.

This fear of contact seems to me to stem largely from the steadily deeper penetration of a money economy, which more and more destroys the natural economic relationships of earlier times (though this work of destruction has not been fully completed). Money is placed between man and man, between man and product, as a mediator, as a general denominator into which every other value must be translated, so that it can be further translated into other values. Since the beginning of a money economy, the objects of economic relationships are no longer immediate to us. Our interest in them is expressed not in their individual and functional meaning, but only through the medium of money. What is their worth, as measured by this intermediary value, meets the eye of *economic* man. Time after time his rational consciousness will stop him at this intermediary step, the center of his interests, his one resting place, while all concrete objects drift by in restless flight. These objects are burdened with a profound contradiction: they alone are able to provide definite satisfactions, yet they obtain their degree of value and interest only after having been evaluated by this yardstick without character and quality. Money, by the enlargement of its role, has placed us at a wider and more basic distance from the object. Immediacy of impression and active interests in things becomes weakened. Our contact with them becomes interrupted, and we sense them only through intermediaries, which can never fully express their genuine, unique and immediate being.

Thus the most diverse features of modern art and culture seem to have in common a deep psychological trait. In abstract terms it may be defined as a tendency to increase the distance between man and his objects, which find its most distinct form in the area of aesthetics. Radical breaks in this tendency, such as naturalism, which seeks conformism with things and absorption in their unbroken reality, must *not* lead us astray. Oscillations between both extremes in particular prove the existence of the same *malaise* from which each of them independently derives. A time which simultaneously idolizes Böcklin and Impressionism, Naturalism and Symbolism, Socialism and Nietzsche—such a time apparently discovers the most developed stimuli of its life in oscillations between the extreme poles of universal human existence. Exhausted nerves which are drifting between hypersensitivity and lack of sensitivity can be excited only by the most opaque forms and rudely accurate details, or else by the most tender and *starkest* stimuli.

Note to the Essay

1. It is an aesthetic question also because of the meaning of the immediate sensation of pleasure and displeasure, and not only on account of the beauty of forms. It would seem harder for a typically "educated" person to overcome the aesthetic discomforts which he experiences during physical contacts with people of the lower class, to whom the honorable sweat of work still clings, than to overcome his attachment to crabmeat, lawn tennis, and easy chairs.

5

On Aesthetic Quantities*

THE ASSUMPTION THAT THE ARTS HAVE NO LIMITS has led a variety of aesthetic movements into the identical error. Abstract idealism is at one with realism in its idea of the relation between art and existence: both believe that, in principle, art can include all subjects within the range of its forms and equip them with equal perfection. This is the extreme opposite of the theory which treats as valid only beautiful and characteristic objects.

The opinion that art can reflect every object accurately, as a mirror, fails to consider that art and artistic media have grown historically. (This artistic pantheism is a form of megalomania which denies relativity and the infinite developmental possibilities of all human affairs.) At different historical points art must have different relationships to the objective being. A characteristic illustration of this will be given here. I will consider the diversity of the aesthetic point of view in its dependence on the diverse and varying physical dimensions of works of art.

Let us consider a postulate which derives from the nature of physical objects: the physical objects demand certain proportions of size for their representation in a work of art. If this postulate and the purely artistic point of view now differ and now coincide, then this does prove that artistic formulations represent very special, accidental, and changing relationships to reality.

The most pronounced discrepancies exist with respect to unorganic nature. For example, paintings of the Alps cannot exhaustively represent their quantitative significance; they appear empty and inadequate. Even

* A translation of "Über aesthetische Quantitäten," *Zeitschrift für pädagogische Psychologie*, 5 (1903), 208–212.

Segantini, the only important painter of Alpine scenes who exists so far, always moved the mountains into the background or chose stylized forms. Moreover, he detracted fully from the demands of this sense impression, which is based primarily on quantitative dimensions, not only by his special treatment of air and of light, but by the quantities of those impressions which could be depicted.

In all organically grown phenomena we find that the circumference always reaches as far as the inner forces are able to develop it. Thus we may have a feeling, through complex, probably unconscious experiences, and through empathy, for the inner forces of growth. Usually therefore, we are in agreement with their size. For the artist, too, the transformations of form which are required because of changes in quantities come about without effort.

In inorganic matters, however, the form does not express inner relationships. There, the forms are molded by exterior forces. The inner principles for the exterior forms, which might guide us in their transformation, are missing. Thus, we can only guide ourselves by the given facts of their spatial dimensions.

How can one explain, furthermore, that individuals without architectural training experience hardly any aesthetic impact from small-scale models of buildings, or at least only an impact which does not do justice to the dimensions of their realistic execution? Psychologically speaking, we are unable to reconstruct imaginatively from such small-scale models relationships of gravity, of weights and supports, of resting and elevating, in short, the dynamic processes. This imaginative intuition develops only with objects of a certain absolute minimum size. This size might be called the threshold of imaginative recall. Our historically given architecture apparently has those quantitative dimensions which permit our soul such an emphatic feeling. As soon as they become smaller or much larger, although we still can view and intellectually consider them, they are devoid of aesthetic effect.

In this context it becomes obvious why idealistic and intellectual aesthetics must necessarily be formalistic. For, whenever importance is placed not on imaginative reconstruction, but on purely intellectual processes, then their conditioning by mere measures of size will be without significance. For pure reason form equals form, and equal forms always must have equal effects.

For some god whose senses were not circumscribed by thresholds of stimuli, size would be completely unimportant. He would not, as we must, connect the qualitative differences of reactions with quantitative differences.

This change of aesthetic values suggests new standards applicable to organic but non-human subject matter. The aesthetic resistance of particular objects is often directed not only against the diminution or enlargement of scale, but sometimes also against their representation in *natural* size. In a not-too-large painting, a horse will always look naturalistic, as if outside the sphere of the work of art. Moreover, certain objects are *a priori* excluded from works of art. It seems that some objects are withheld from artistic reproduction in the same measure in which interest in their *reality* dominates the imagination associatively, as for example the concerns of routine daily life, extremely remarkable phenomena and accidents, and more of the like.

All these phenomena drive the category of being into consciousness as a question, a wish, or knowledge. Thereby, however, they remove themselves from the merely idealistic sphere of art.

This series of motives can also be augmented from another direction. A rider on horseback produces a contradiction if he is rendered in natural size, since his life-size representation will have realistic effects. The inner and justified relationship of these two appears directly reversed. A diminution, however, would shift the artistic relationship of the parts to favor the spiritually higher. This suggests that the individual parts of a work of art are effective not only through their mutual relationships, but that a certain absolute size of the whole work of art is required which alone will give the proper meaning to those relations. The accent may be placed on the form, but the potential of being able to decide is only reached once it appears in a certain scale.

The human figure presents an aesthetic miracle insofar as it maintains its aesthetic value through almost all possible enlargements and diminutions of scale. The reason for this is that its aesthetic proportions, with which we are in *solidarity*, take on such importance and concreteness for us, and have such immediate inner necessity, that they dominate everything else. Indeed, the human figure is perceived as a norm for the qualities and proportions of everything else: man is the measure of all things also in visual matters.

When we are dealing with relationships among human beings, however, the problem of quantities, however, arises once again. For example, in paintings of Madonnas, the child in its bodily smallness contradicts his dominant central role. The childlike form, with its limited potential of differentiation, is hardly suited to express spiritually important matters. This problem has been completely overcome only in the Sistine Madonna.

There are no limits to the power of the artist. By saying this, however, it is not implied that the quantitative dependence is insignificant. It only means that size is one element which may be overcome by other elements, but which will not disappear. Each artistically usable element seems to be composed of two thresholds of size. There is a certain quantity for their representation through which aesthetic reactions in the final analysis are produced, and there is one through which they disappear again. Such thresholds can also be found in other spheres of the higher mental life as, for example, the threshold of becoming conscious of justice [1] or of religion.

These aesthetic thresholds of objects, which determine their utilization for aesthetic purposes, are moved together or apart in accordance with the artist's potential concerning form. With a growing refinement of aesthetic knowledge, however, the threshold values must approximate one another more and more. Finally, if we should ever attain complete knowledge concerning artistic composition, we will develop a definite scale for measuring the full artistic impression.

The one conclusion of all previous studies concerning these problems is that certain modifications of aesthetic response can be explained by merely quantitative changes. This, however, only formulates the problem. The psychological connections are still missing.

To this subject I shall now contribute two ideas. The first concerns not so much the size of a work of art as the amount of emotional excitement it evokes. To judge the importance of a work of art simply by the quantity of sensation it generates is extremely dilettantish. To provide a valid standard, the emotional force with which the audience is carried along must remain formally consistent with respect to rhythmical balance. Neither must the quantity of impressions be allowed to transgress a certain level, or else our emotional responses will drown out our artistic ones.

For example, when we read a novel, the tension which is often produced in us by an overdeveloped interest in its subject matter may destroy its artistic effect. A certain distance and reserve are necessary. We are dealing here with a question of quantity; even if we were already familiar with the content, its artistic form would nevertheless generate a tension and empathy in us, but it would compare with the previously mentioned realistic impressions only as a tender image. The arts, so to speak, seem to present us with the content of life without representing life itself.

Thus it seems to me that the strength of emotion also has an upper and a lower aesthetic threshold. Beyond the one, there is apathy; beyond the other there is realistic participation. This displacement of the quantitative aspect of sensations means not only that there is room for the aesthetic feeling, but that this more abstract emotional force, which is not short of the quality of realistic feelings, already by itself represents an aesthetic quality. Under whatever circumstances we otherwise recognize diminutions in the intensity of feelings, we seem to perceive a lack of success, a failure. Only the arts seem to know how to conserve without gaps the complete *cosmos* of feelings.

Our second consideration concerns the value of quantities in the most external meaning of the term. It seems to us to be self-evident that subjects which have very important inner meanings will require a larger-size canvas, while less important subjects require a smaller one. This relationship is not at all self-evident. It seems to stem from the fact that the size of any given image requires a certain part of our visual field. If a picture does not completely fill the visual field or fills it almost fully, then inevitably many other objects will also be seen. A proper relationship between the sense of content and totality of the interests of the moment is needed. Further, complete sensuous aware-ness should be demanded only by an aesthetically important subject. A less important one should not be permitted to pre-empt the whole field of vision. This would violate all symbolism, which is the essence of art.

The final observation concerning perfection in art is that art knows how to obey the postulates of objects which develop independently of one another with equal justice and balance; thus what is real has the choice only of which one it should follow, as if there were only a single law which separates what is real into coincidence and apathetic alienation.

Thus we see that there are demands on the quantitative dimen-sions of a work of art which derive, on the one hand, from purely artistic conditions and, on the other, from our bodily and mental struc-tures. From the intrinsic meanings of objects (associations—inner mean-ings) flow others which, however, coincide with the former although they are not restrained by any pre-established harmony.

Thus art shows us the unified context of its elements in the image of being, which reality seems to keep from us. This unity, however, cannot be foreign to our deepest understanding, since the *image* of being must finally also be a *part* of being.

Note to the Essay

1. *De minimis non curat praetor.* (Roman Law: The praetor does not con-cern himself with trifles.)

6

On the Third Dimension in Art*

T HE DESIRE WE FIND AMONG RECENT PAINTERS to portray *the third dimension* in two-dimensional pictures is not natural or imperative to their art form. We can observe that both the finest nuances of sensual perception and the most extreme poles of emotional expression can be reached without it. Consider, for example, the women of the Japanese painters Harunobu and Utamaro, whose souls, like their bodies, appear as blossoms waving in the summer wind, or, in another vein, Aubrey Beardsley's degrading perversities and satanic expressions. Why then should some painters strive so avidly for a third dimension? It cannot be simply a more realistic reproduction of nature that they seek: nature must inevitably be distorted in being transformed into art. Moreover, the purposes of art are fulfilled through much simpler means than nature employs. Thus, realistic elements do not in themselves have artistic value; they must legitimize themselves by other means.

The very special meaning which the dimension of depth has stems from the fact that, in contrast to the other two dimensions, it is not optically evident. Only our tactile sense convinces us that bodies embody more than their two-dimensional surface. The full image of things, which results from their being visible and the possibility of their being touched, is reproduced by its visibility. Hence, it appears to us as if we immediately perceived the third dimension. In reality things are being touched continuously, and the associative effects of our sense of touch on visual perception are, or in principle could be, continuously controlled. Thus, the third dimension in painting depends much more on visual images than the third dimension in reality, for in art

* A translation of "Über die dritte Dimension in der Kunst," *Zeitschrift für Aesthetik*, 1 (1906), 65–69.

there is absolutely no other point of reference besides purely optical processes. For this reason the third dimension appears as a world separated in principle from the actually given visual impression. In order for the visual impression to convey the third dimension, it must appear to us with much greater power. It acts like a mystic exorcism which attempts to dominate an object with which it is denied any direct contact. I see an essentially effective value in this complete exclusion of any direct participation by the tactile sense on which the imagination of the third dimension properly rests. And yet I see also its simultaneous inclusion in the visual impression.

A fact that is very simple yet fundamentally significant emerges from this. In principle any given art form affects only one human sense, while on the other hand every "real" object affects, or can affect, a plurality of senses. In this way "reality" is made. A body which we could not only see, but penetrate without experiencing a tactile sensation could not be considered "real," but would be ghostlike. The same consideration applies to an object which we might touch but which would not produce a sound when it collides with another object, or similarly, a sound which radiated from a source that could not be seen or otherwise located. It is characteristic of reality that a plurality of sensual impressions meet in it, fix it, as if by a system of coordinates. Simultaneously, however, each sense gives an object a qualitatively unique world of its own which has no substantive contact with any other object. That it is one and the same object which I see and touch represents a synthesis of postulates or categories which are by themselves of an order different from sensual images. Within reality the object is created by the equal cooperation of completely independent and mutually alien conditions. The essence of a work of art, however, is determined by its very opposition to this process. Aesthetic contemplation has an integrity which can never be provided by perception of reality, because the work of art appears exclusively as the product of a single sense. This single sense takes over the autocratic leadership in the mixture of flowing reproductions, which consequently become ranked and organized beyond comparison. By this hierarchy the complete determination of the senses is prevented. Thus, where a multitude of sense impressions are fused in "real" man, who can be touched, heard, and smelled, a work of art is arrested in the sphere of nonreality by the fact that its impact derives exclusively from a *single* sense. Thus, in works of art the third dimension of the tactile sense, the domain of the proper "sense of reality," plays a role completely different from that in impressions of reality.

In the realm of plastic art these conditions are only apparently different. Marble, of course, can be touched, but it is not by itself a work of art—just as a canvas and its layers of paint which can be touched do not make of it a painting. For the inartistic observer a statue is a human figure made from marble, just as a living human being to him represents one made of flesh and bones. In this sense, of course, both are "real" since they can be touched. However, a body which in truth becomes an object of art cannot be touched. Nor can the body in a painting be touched since it is only represented in the tactile, real material [of the canvas], just as the body in the painting is not contained in the touchable specks of paint. The third dimension is without relation to the work of art since here the tactile sense guarantees the realism of the object. It is only related to a work of art insofar as the eye is stimulated by the mere apperception of a plastic work to the production or reproduction of the dimension of depth. The plastic work of art exists only to be viewed, and not in order to be touched. Since the third dimension can only be sensed by touch, by directly ascertaining that it is a piece of marble, it necessarily must belong in a completely different area from the artistic meaning of marble. The third dimension enters into this area of meaning only after it is, so to speak, reborn through its genuine tactile value as a product of visual impressions.

I do not mean to deny the role of what Berenson called *tactile values*. Nevertheless, it is still necessary to determine what gives the capacity to evoke sensations of resistance and their modification, an aesthetic significance which increases the artistic value to a painting. Why, for example, is something added to the artistic stimulus of a painted column, which would seem to be exhausted by the visibility of its form and color, when its coldness and harshness is psychologically considered? Or, what is being added to painted silk when its sheen also reproduces the sensation of the material with its mixture of spryness and softness? I do not think that this addition of concurrent perceptions in itself has aesthetic significance. On the contrary, I believe, its aesthetic value comes from the transformation of tactile impressions by optical impressions. This is no different from music, which also calls forth in us innumerable reproductions from all spheres of life whose whole and unique charm and depth consist only in the fact that they are transformed into music. They accompany the movement of sounds, not as their mechanical equivalents, but through specific reformulations and recolorations. They have to undergo an allotropic modification in order to become the satellites of musical impressions from which they would otherwise stand estranged, belonging to a different order of things.

The memories of other senses would only be dragged along as a strange appendage by the visual impression, without enriching and deepening its meaning, if they were nothing but naturalistic repetitions of their former content. In order to enter the unity of works of art, they must transform their original meaning, which has nothing to do with the present meaning, into perceptual values. Or, they must transform their being, which is originally quite differently structured, so that it will enter into an organic unity with the optical artistic impression. It is in the preliminary form of a mere postulate that we psychologically describe this expatriation of the tactile senses by their inclusion into art. At any rate, one is then able to describe this process as a change in quality of visual perception—or on a different level as a change of tactile perceptions. It is not possible to deduce the artistic meaning of tactile values from mere associations, insofar as the latter can only represent merely unorganic and unfruitful changes in the quantity of inner processes. When, for example, the sensations produced by one's touching silk influence one's perception of the painted material, this perception as such becomes deeper, more vivid, and more extensive. This transmutation of heterogeneous sensual impressions into optical values was known to Goethe: ". . . und durchs Auge schleicht die Kühle sänftigend ins Herz hinein." * The object thus offers more to the eye. This does not apply so much with respect to reality, where the diverse senses maintain their special values, since they all contribute equally to the reality of objects. It applies especially to works of art which reduce the content of perceived phenomena to the general denominator of a single sense. Similarly, it probably applies to the third dimension, which represents everything that tactile values have in common. The touched surfaces possess, in addition to harshness and softness, roughness and smoothness, pointedness and balanced shape, the general quality of resistance to touch, which adds to the very surface—which is also presented to the eye—the third dimension. If the latter is to enter into the pure visual work of art, it will not merely be as another dimension, a mere numerical addition to the already present quantum of dimensions. Instead, it will add a new note of quality to the already present [number] which the work of art cannot transcend.

In painting and plastic art, the third dimension does not provide a real extension in depth, but an enrichment and reinforcement of the two-dimensional pictorial content. This is so since something which is eternally invisible cannot have any place in the domain of sensual perception. Here it appears as a nuance of visibility which the organizing perception of the artist has transformed by the addition of experience and associations from the worlds of other senses. Finally, this transformation of the mere addition, which the third dimension can contribute to the other two dimensions, subordinates itself to the mean-

* Through the eye, coolness soothingly enters the heart.

89

ing of all art in its relationship to natural science. While the latter attempts to reduce all qualities to quantitative expressions, that is, to portray them according to their meaning in quantitative terms, art, on the contrary, attempts to describe everything that exists only in quantitative dimensions in its appropriate meaning of quality.

7

The Dramatic Actor and Reality*

A S UNCERTAIN AND CRITICAL as one may be of "public opinion," that is, the *vox populi*, generally there is a core of relevant and reliable content in the dark premonitions, instincts, and evaluations of the masses. Obviously this core is surrounded by a thick shell of superficial trivialities and biased information. Nevertheless, its fundamental accuracy will usually become apparent in the realms of religion and politics, or in intellectual and ethical matters. Only in one area, the field of the art, which appears to be even more accessible than others, is the judgment of the masses hopelessly misguided and completely inadequate, especially with respect to fundamental issues. An abyss without bridges cuts off the majority from insight into the essence of art forms. Therein rests the deep social tragedy of art.

In the dramatic arts, which appeal more directly to a public audience than any other, genuine artistic values seem to be sprung not from the intentions of the artist, but from the immediate impression he makes on the audience. Because of this democratized mass appeal, dramatic art would seem to be more profoundly naturalistic than any other art form. Thus public opinion sees the essence of dramatic art not in the written drama, but in the dramatic actor.

A dramatic play exists as a self-contained work of art. Does the contribution of the actor now elevate this play into an art form of greater magnitude? If this question seems inappropriate, we might rephrase it. Does the actor transform the work of art to a more convincing level through his physical, live appearance? But, if this is true, why do we demand that his performance should somehow bear the imprint

* A translation of "Der Schauspieler und die Wirklichkeit," in Georg Simmel, *Brücke und Tür*, ed. Margarete Susman and Michael Landmann (Stuttgart: K. F. Koehler Verlag, 1957), pp. 168–175.

of art, and not simply that of mere realistic naturalism? All the problems dealing with the philosophy of the dramatic art converge on these questions.

The role of the actor, as it is expressed in written drama, is not a total person. The role is not a man, but a complex of things which can be said about a person through literary devices. The poet cannot give the actor unambiguous instructions concerning the inflection of language, the tone of voice, or the pace of delivery. He can only project the fate, the appearance, and the soul of a person through the one-dimensional process of poetic imagery. The actor then translates this image into a three-dimensional character accessible to all the senses.

The actor's essential mistake is to identify the sensual interpretation of an artistic content with its full realization. For the ultimate realization of drama is a metaphysical idea which cannot be embodied through sensuous impressions. The content which the poet molds into a dramatic script reveals completely different connotations when transformed into sensuous expression. The actor gives meaning to the script, but he does not transform its content into reality. This is why his acting can become art, which, by definition, reality could never be. Thus, if painting appears as the art of visual sensuality and music as the art of acoustic sensuality, dramatic art appears as the art form of total sensuality.

In the realm of reality every single element and event is placed in an infinitely expanding series of spatial, conceptual, and dynamic relationships. For this reason every identifiable element of reality is only a fragment and not a totality. It is the nature of art, on the other hand, to mold the contents of existence into self-contained unity. The actor raises *all* the visual and acoustical elements of reality into a perfectly framed unity. This is accomplished through the balance of style, the logic of rhythm, the movement of moods, the recognizable relationship between character and action, and through the subordination of all details under the apex of the whole. The actor thus stylizes all sensual phenomena into a unity.

At this point reality seems again to penetrate the realm of the arts in order to bridge a void. How does the actor acquire the mode of conduct appropriate to his role when, as we have seen, this mode is not explicit in the script and cannot be made so? It seems to me that the actor cannot know how to perform Hamlet except through his own experience. He will rely on external and (more important) inner experience to realize how a human being who talks like Hamlet and has encountered Hamlet's fate generally behaves. Thus the actor submerges himself in the foundations of reality from which Shakespeare originally had derived the role. From this he recreates the dramatic work of art, in the form of Hamlet. The dramatic composition guides the actor by providing a system of realistic coordinates corresponding to the individual's inner and outer experiences, reactions, fates, events, and their environmental surroundings. However, regardless of how much guidance he might get from the play, he could not understand its clues unless he had been empirically acquainted with them or similar ones already. At this point the contribution of naturalism ends. Besides the written words of Shakespeare concerning Hamlet, the actor only has empirical reality with which to reconstruct everything Shakespeare did not say. Thus, he has to behave like a real Hamlet who has been restricted by the words and events prescribed for him by Shakespeare.

But this argument is quite erroneous. The activity of giving artistic form and constructing the artistic imprint transcends that reality on which the actor leans under the guidance of the script. The actor does not content himself with empirical reality. The coordinates of reality must become reallocated: accents become toned down, measures of time become subjected to rhythm, and from all the alternatives offered by reality, only those that can be uniformly stylized are selected. In short, the actor does not transform the dramatic work of art into reality; on the contrary, he makes use of reality, and transforms the reality which has been assigned to him into a work of art.

There are many sophisticated people today who explain their aversion towards the theater by saying that it portrays too many artificial pretenses. This opinion may be justified, not because of a shortage of reality, but because of a surfeit of it. The dramatic actor can be convincing to us only if he stays within artistic logic, and eschews additional elements of realism obeying a completely different logic.

It is wrong to consider it a "falsification" if the actor is different in reality from the role he assumes on stage. After all, no one charges a locomotive engineer with falsifying himself if he fails to run locomotives around his family table. It is not a deception when the penniless actor assumes the role of a king on stage. For he is a king in his function as an artist, an *ideal* king, but perhaps for this very reason, not a *real* king. This impression of falsehood is generated only by a poor actor, who either permits traces of his role in reality as a poor individual to enter into his stage role of a king, or else acts so very realistically that he carries us into the sphere of realism. In the latter case he creates a painful competition between two realistic images which contradict one another. This contradiction would never occur if the dramatic presentation kept the audience in the sphere of art, which is essentially estranged from reality.

We now see the total error in the idea that the actor must realize the poetic creation. In the dramatic presentation the actor exercises a special and unified form of art which is as far removed from reality as the poetic work of art itself. Thus we can immediately understand why a good imitator is not a good actor. The gift of being able to imitate other people has nothing to do with the artistically creative talent of an actor. This is true because the subject matter of the imitator is reality, and thus he strives to be received as a form of reality. The actor, however, like the painter of a portrait, is not the imitator of the real world, but the creator of a new one. This artistic world, of course, is related to the phenomenon of reality, since both the real and artistic worlds are built on the accumulated content of all being. Reality, however, represents the first impression received of these contents. This stimulates the illusion, as though reality was the true subject of art.

In order to obtain the most refined method of keeping the dramatic arts in the sphere of reality, the dramatic writer derives his material from his psychological integration of previous experience. The words of the poet demand a reconstruction based on psychological experience. The task of the actor should make us conceive of the prescribed words and events as inevitable. Thus, his art should be applied or *practical* psychology. According to this view, the task of the actor is fulfilled by placing before our eyes convincingly and emphatically the essence of a human soul with its inner determination, its reaction to fate, its drives, and its emotional anguish.

The proper artistic contribution of the dramatic actor cannot be found in the apparent depth of his interpretation. Certainly it is only through his own spiritual experiences that an actor can understand the role of Hamlet. Moreover, the actor would only be a puppet or a phonograph if he were not able to represent this spiritual reality to the viewer for a chance to experience it, too. However, true art transcends this experience of a reproduced psychic reality. It flows from an ideal fountain, from the beginning, never towards a finished reality, but towards new demands.

We see here a revival, new in aesthetics, of the old error overcome long ago in philosophy—the idea that mental reality is something transcendent, ideal, superior to physical reality. Art, however, demands that the mere causality of factual processes should explicate meanings, that all the threads which extend into infinity of time and place should be laced together into a self-satisfactory whole, and that the confusion of reality should be rhythmically ordered. These demands do not correspond to the reality that flows from the dark fountain of being, inaccessible to our consciousness, even if this reality were of a psychic variety.

There is no doubt that these postulates concerning art originate in the minds of real human beings, as do ideas about the appropriate relation between the form and the content of reality. However, the content and meaning of the artistic work is juxtaposed in one's mind with the reality which the mind reconstructs from experience. The dramatic actor must make us understand the role of Hamlet and portray the turmoils of his fate. Through his gestures and the pitch and rhythm of his voice, he must also provide us with psychological insight, so that we all draw the conclusion that a given character *must* speak these words under the given circumstances. The genuine artistic process, however, only begins after all this has happened—after the role of Hamlet is made into more than a series of resounding words and exterior events, and has been resolved through the contribution of the actor into a spiritual reality which contrasts with the immediacy of excitement and empathy. Here the spiritually recreated process of reality crystallizes into an image. This is analogous to the sensually perceived impressions of the world of physical bodies which are transformed by the painter into a painting. This spiritual reality has thus become a picture for the dramatic writer.

We can now formulate these ideas into an axiom: *The dramatic arts as such transcend both poetry and reality.* The dramatic actor is neither what popular naturalism demands, an imitator of a man who finds himself in a given situation, nor what literary idealism demands, a marionette of his role with no artistic task besides what is already prescribed in the lines of the poetic work.

This literary point of view is particularly seductive to naturalism. If one does not permit the dramatic actor an individual contribution, produced according to autonomous artistic principles based on the final foundations of all art, then the actor becomes only the *realization* of a written role. A work of art, however, cannot be the material subject for another work of art. On the contrary, a dramatic play is a channel through which a stream, flowing from the very fundamentals of being, is directed towards the specifically individual artistic contribution of the dramatic actor. If it were otherwise, there would be no other final principles then those of drama and reality. On such a basis, then, the actor's task could only be considered dangerously close to naturalism, namely, to provide the appearance of reality for the dramatic play.

The attractive notion that the dramatic actor only infuses the dramatic play with life, and presents the life realization of a poetic work, leads to the disappearance of the genuine and incomparable dramatic art which lives in the realm between the written play and reality. It is just as distinctively *original* to represent elements of life through the medium of dramatic acting as to represent them through painting or poetry, or to recreate them through epistemology or religion. And the art form of the dramatic actor is something which is genuinely rooted in unity, despite the great variety of sensuous impressions and emotional reactions that it produces. It is not a composite of independent optical stimuli, acoustic rhythms, emotional shocks, or states of empathy. On the contrary, dramatic acting represents an inner unity produced from the diversity of all those great elements of which the dramatic impressions seem to be composed. In reality, they are only developments from a single root, just as the multitude of different words in a sentence represent a single pattern of thought. There simply seems to exist an *attitude of dramatic acting* which man brings into this world as part of his manner of being and which makes him creative in this unique way.

The decisive point is the fact that the dramatic actor creates within himself a complete unity with its unique laws. His art, just as that of the poet, has its roots in the same fundamentals as do all other art forms. This is true even though it demands another art form, the poetic work, for its medium. Only the autonomous status of the dramatic art explains the strange fact that a poetic role, although conceived as an unambiguous one, can be presented by a variety of dramatic actors with completely different interpretations, each of which may be fully adequate, and none of which would be more correct or more erroneous than any other. This would be completely incomprehensible if the dramatic actor lived entirely within the dualism between the poetic work and reality. Within the frameworks of both the poetic role and reality (which might be thought of as the poetic counter-image), there exists only *one* Don Carlos or *one* Gregers Werle. Without a third, genuine, independent foundation, this separation of the various branches of the dramatic arts would lead to the destruction of the unities existing both within poetic works and within reality.

Thus dramatic acting is not, as is commonly thought, the reconciliation between the realism of poetry and reality. Nor is it the servant of those two lords. The accuracy with which the dramatic actor follows the poetic role, and the truth of the given world, are not mechanical copies of each other. Rather, the dramatic actor's personality interweaves those two roles as organic elements in his creative expression of life. He was born as a personality and not with a predetermined dependence on written dramatic works, or with a reality which he is expected to redraft.

Here we find one more example of an important historic task which confronts the present age: to replace mechanism with life processes. We have come to see how each individual's reality contains in itself a condensation of life, which determines its essence and includes in its development all those living realizations which surround it in organic interdependence. The mechanical principle, on the other hand, de-individualizes all these phenomena and reconstructs them, more or less externally, as mere combinations of others. If we understand the dramatic art as an expression of the primary artistic energy of the human soul, which assimilates both the poetic art and reality into one living process, instead of being composed of these elements in a mechanical fashion, then our interpretation of this art coincides with our distinctively modern way of understanding the modern world.

8

Psychological and Ethnological Studies on Music*,¹

I

DARWIN WRITES in *The Descent of Man:* "We must suppose that the rhythms and cadences of oratory are derived from previously developed musical powers. We can thus understand how it is that music, dancing, song, and poetry are such very ancient arts. We may go even further then this and believe that musical sounds afforded one of the bases for the development of language." ² In similar fashion he elaborates in his work, *On the Expression of the Emotions,*³ his view that the singing of birds serves especially the purpose of mating calls. It expresses sexual drives and charms the females. Man supposedly first used his voice for this purpose, and not in verbal language, which Darwin sees as one of the most recent products of human development. On the other hand, the use of musical tones for the attraction of females (or conversely of males) can be observed among animals of a very low order. Jaeger likewise observes that the singing of birds is not all that intimately related to articulated verbal language.⁴ On the contrary, it corresponds precisely to the unarticulated wordless yodeling of man. It is "the expressive sound of sexual excitement, the tones of pleasure." But the meaning of birds singing should be more broadly interpreted, because it is also used to express pleasures derived from other sources, such as sunshine or the discovery of food. One should keep in mind, of course, that warmth and certain food items can also be stimulants.

* A translation of "Psychologische und ethnologische Studien über Musik," *Zeitschrift für Völkerpsychologie und Sprachwissenschaft,* 13 (1882), 261–305.

Human yodeling, however, is also connected with the sexual sphere, since it is said to be the sign of communication between boy and girl.

I should like to reply to these views that every expression of birds is vocal in nature. Just as birds express every other emotion through singing, so they must also express their sexual feelings. Even if these conditions were the most powerful, all others could rightfully serve for the same analogy. If this were so, it would be hard to understand why man should have progressed to verbal language, since he could express everything through the use of tones. Now I will even adopt Darwin's point of view: if man had found this non-verbal use of the singing voice, which he is said to have inherited from his ancestors, more natural than language, would he not have maintained it on the lowest cultural level as a survival, so that contemporary man, too, would express himself by worldless yodeling? With the exception of our mountain people, however, there is no evidence of its anywhere else in the world, as Professor Bastian assured me and as I convinced myself in my own studies. We will have occasion to examine this yodeling, of dubious sexual connection, later (see Section XVII of this study). For birds, of course, singing is the natural expression of emotions, while man is more likely to shout. Why should man have searched for another form of expression for such a natural emotion as the sexual drive?

The priority of vocal singing over verbal language seems to me to be undemonstrable. Nor am I persuaded by the other argument that children are more likely in this fashion to imitate singing than speech. (A mother of five children, who later turned out to be musically talented, told me that none of her children sang in tones before their second or third years.) I believe that the reason for this is simply that children hardly understand the meaning of presented words. If they repeat anything, it is simply mechanical. The children must memorize the series of phonemes in order to reproduce them. Obviously this is difficult, and it is much easier for him to memorize and reproduce the speech melody, which makes a more precise sensual impression than the phonemes. If the speech melody now takes on a vocal melody, the child will naturally be able to imitate it more easily, since it will make an even more precise impression. It is only because it is mechanically easier to imitate the melody that it will be repeated by the child more readily than will the words. This would prove only that a child commences singing without words. But so far it has not been proven that the child will do so without imitating. Casual singing without words is only observed among adults, never among very small children, who always sing words.

The role which is played by the memory in this connection can be seen from the following: consider a child who is able to repeat a simple folk melody. Now, if one sings for him one of Chopin's melodies, which consists of the identical selection of tones, only in different sequence, he will not be able to repeat it. Obviously this is because, just as in adults, the memory has not been able to retain this less natural sequence of tones. The child's technical capacity for reproducing these sounds is demonstrated by his repeating the folk song. The custom of ancient peoples who usually sang their legal texts before the invention of phonetic writing can probably be attributed to their unconscious awareness of the greater security in reproduction that results from connecting text with melody. Here we are dealing not simply with the facilitation of serial reproductions which would be the consequences of their temporal sequence. On the contrary, each individual element—or at least each group of elements—enters into a substantively founded synthesis with the corresponding one of the other sequences. This also demonstrates the basic relationship between poetry and music. As is well-known, the memory retains rhythmic and rhymed material much more easily than it does prose, and for a longer time.

II

It seems most likely to me that the source of vocal music is the spoken word, which is exaggerated by emotions in the direction of rhythm and modulation. My reasons are as follows. Language and mind develop through mutual support and strengthening. The progress of the one is built upon that of the other. "The essence of man is thought, and human thought is originally language," says Steinthal. Therefore, wherever there are psychic processes among man, there is also language. Man's drive to express inner emotions through external action, which previously could only be satisfied by gestures and shouting, is given a richer and more appropriate form through language. This linguistic bridge from animal to human being cannot be retraced. Every emotion searches for expression in more and more characteristic linguistic form. Thinking and feeling among aborigines is expressed through speech. "Children and primitives speak almost continuously," observes Lazarus. More refined and emphatic psychic processes will search for a more exaggerated expression. Acute and intense processes will be very strong. For this reason the linguistic ability of primitive people will not provide an equivalent compensation for it, be it ever so intensified and expressive. For example, sudden terror will only cause us to scream, as will intense pain.[5] On the other hand, there are emotions which will not be strong enough to overcome the drive for linguistic expression. Nevertheless, they will not be able to find an adequate compensation in the usual modes and forms of language. Anger, for example, finds expression in words, but with an intensified accentuation of voice level that is a far louder than usual one. Depression is expressed through words of softer and more monotonous character. There may also be additional emotions which amplify the rhythmic and modulatory elements of language. One example is the activities of war. The intensification of energies on this occasion seems to infuse all activities with rhythmic expression, as shown in the dancing and rhythmic steps used by many primitive peoples. When primitive man has progressed so far that he expresses his emotions through language (he must already have reached this stage when he engages in organized warfare)—so that, for example, specific expressions have been developed in a tribe for specific situations (for example, calls for bravery and for deprecating the enemy in warfare)—he then produces these sounds rhythmically and in keeping with the whole disposition and in step. Through the teaching of ethnology, we know that these rhythmically organized sounds are practiced throughout the world at the approach of the enemy. Rhythm, indeed, is the very beginning of music.

A second cause of the evolution of vocal song may have been a diffuse feeling of pleasure and enjoyment. We observe that people are more talkative when in happy spirits than when they are in quiet or depressed moods. Children especially, even when they are by themselves, will be observed speaking continuously when they are enjoying themselves. Primitive man, however, will employ the same words for all forms of emotional expression, only he will vary the tonal pitch and emphasis for expressions of joy. While his language has, as yet, not rigidified toward stabilized speech melody, he has at his disposal the fullness of modulation and differentiation.[6]

Even today we alter our mode of speech when we express joyful emotions. We then deflect our speech melody and produce a more melodious and harmonic speech pattern, as if we wished to give evidence of our inner harmony. Furthermore, one should observe that there seems to be a tendency towards rhythmic expression whenever we are happy. This is so, most likely, not only because there is an intrinsic link between rhythm and melody formation, but also for substantive reasons. The rhythmic motions of the dance are, among others, reproductions of the joyful mood.[7]

In this category of emotions we may also include the sexual drive. I believe that I have already shown that it is impossible to prove in this manner the non-verbal origin of music. It may be possible, as Jaeger suggests, that the sexual excitement which accompanies verbal courting led, by its exaggeration, to vocal music (see Sections I and XVIII of this study). But then, one has to disregard the most primitive means known for satisfying the sexual drive, abduction, since it is not at all connected with courting. It is impossible to show that human singing is anywhere used merely as an animalistic expression. To this point, as to many others, Wilhelm Von Humboldt has added another seed of wisdom. He says,

> Words flow from the heart freely without necessity or intention. There may not have been in a desolate area any nomadic hunting horde which did not already own its own songs, for man, as an animal species, is a singing creature. He does, however, *connect thoughts with sound.*[8]

A fourth emotion may be mentioned among the sources of vocal music: the mystical-religious. Almost all incantations, magic formulas, and prayers, as far as we can trace them in ethnographic materials, are produced with the greatest possible pathos, which approximates the tonal pattern of vocal music the most closely. Even today, speech is produced nowhere else in a more singing fashion than from the pulpit and during prayers. Indeed the ordinary begging tone noticeably approximates singing.[9] Also, the rhythmical element must be emphasized by the well-measured and elongated forms that are germane to mysticism. This is also demonstrated by the dance, which is employed in every primitive religion to express religious emotion.

The languages of Negro tribes supposedly consist almost exclusively of continuous recitations. The reason for this is certainly the easy excitability of these people, their emotional devotion and dedication to all fleeting ideas and impressions, so that the excitement at any given moment is probably too strong to be expressed in simple words, and therefore takes refuge in musical exaggeration. When in contrast to our harsh sounding idioms it has been said that the language of Greeks and Italians sound more like music, then his inclination to melody in speech is certainly not without connection to the more excited and simultaneously more emotional character of these people. What is commonly called musical talent of individuals and whole societies may, therefore, be derivable from such more general psychological qualities.

It seems to me that the first form of song stemmed from such origins. This first form, however, was quite different from what we today conceive of as vocal music. But one must not forget that music in this state was not yet art, just as the huts of the primitive people were not works of architectural art. In order for them to be developed into a form of art, a special impetus was needed which was not wholly conditioned by these first origins. No traveler has hesitated to recognize the songs of primitive peoples as music despite their unbelievable monotony or lack of harmony. Ammian describes the war songs of Bardal as songs, even though he compares their sound with the noise of the ocean when it beats against rocks. That the Chinese say, when they listen to European songs, that "the dogs are howling here," is characteristic of the difference in judgment concerning what is real and proper music. To European ears, Chinese music is equally incomprehensible. If, then, in our own time when music by no means approximates pure or natural sound any more, such differences in judgment occur—so that something can now be regarded as song and soon again be rejected— how much more must the boundaries between shouting, words and singing have vacillated during primeval days when the tonal material was in a more fluid condition. The reason that singing approximates unarticulated shouting more closely than spoken words seems to lie in the fact that whenever a larger number of untrained and uneducated individuals congregate for singing, the result, even today, is usually closer to noise than to musical tones.[10] Moreover, whenever excitement reaches a climax, vocal singing may not be an adequate compensation for these emotions, so that one has to resort to shouting. "Voluntary interjections are only employed when the suddenness or vehemence of some affection or passion returns men to their natural state." [11]

Concerning this transition from speaking to singing and from singing to shouting, it is interesting to note what Freycinet tells about the savage people of Rio de Janeiro during the period of European contact.

> They used to celebrate a religious festival every three to four years, during which the magicians named Caraibes separated the people into men, women, and children, and placed them in three separate buildings. The magicians entered the house of the men, whereupon all those assembled began to speak in low tones. Then they sang in a higher tone, whereupon the woman responded to these songs with a trembling voice. Soon they shouted with force, then they rose violently up to the point of frothing. . . .[12]

A similar rise is mentioned by Hochstetter concerning the love songs of the Maori.

> The refrain of each verse is formed by violently ejaculated guttural sounds. Through this manner of presentation the intention of drawing an adequate picture of the vehement emotions which capture the whole man is fulfilled.[13]

With respect to this transition of speech to song, Martius observes that

> . . . whenever a Botucotu tribesman desires or demands something longingly, or attains an emotional state, he will raise his speech to a

monotonous song. It seems as if he wanted to replace the meagerness of his expression with the increased volume of sound.[14]

Grey observes exactly the same among the Australian aborigines.[15] The Tehuelche people let their songs be heard only during their festivities and while they are drunk. It resembles their speech patterns closely, and is apparently a transition of speech into song, which is the result of the agitation of the moment.[16]

It seems to me, therefore, that vocal music must have developed from speech. Originally it was only language which was exaggerated by emotional states.[17] Our linguistic usage retains some signs of this relationship insofar as the most sophisticated form of language, namely poetry, is described as song. One should pay attention to how closely the voice approaches song whenever a poem is presented with fullest dedication to emotion and declaimed with pathos. Indeed, at some distance one might be tempted to mistake it for a monotonous song.[18] But it is just as monotonous as are the songs of almost all primitive peoples of whom we have knowledge.

It follows from the nature of vocal music that the more closely related it is with poetry, the closer it is to its origin. Bodenstedt tells of the song-loving Caucasian soldiers.

> I had some of the major singers come to me and dictate some of the songs which had appealed to me the most. It was, however, impossible to get the Kerle (fellows) to the point where they would sing to me a song word for word. They hummed and sang on and on. Usually they had already finished with the whole song before I had completed the transcription of the first verse. I let them know that presently I was not interested in the melody, but that they should tell me the texts word for word. They attempted their best to comply with my wish, but it was impossible for them to *utter one verse in this fashion.* Finally one of them said, "Sir, such things one cannot simply say, they must be sung." [19]

I do not need to remind the reader here of the innermost fusion of the two during classic antiquity. I will cite only a single passage which seems to me especially characteristic: "The very rocks of the wilderness give back a sympathetic echo to the voice; savage beasts have sometimes been charmed into stillness by song; and shall we, who are nurtured upon all that is highest, be deaf to the appeal of poetry?" [20] Cicero is referring here to Orpheus, of whom it is reported that he tamed wild beasts by the sound of pure music. Nowhere is it said that they understood the content or words of the poems he sang. With this reference Cicero intends to defend Archias, who was only a poet and needed never to have sung a note during his whole life. The concepts, however, of poetry and song are so closely related (the one infallibly calls for the other) that without much reflection the essence and effects of both become identified even though there may not be any direct relationships between the two.

III

The variety of idiomatic expressions in which the continuous repetition of similar parts is compared with music indicates how very characteristic rhythm is for music, namely, the repetition of similar structures. See for example sayings such as: You shall be deprived, deprived you shall be, so goes the eternal song. The old round. In the same meaning: the old song. *C'est toujours la même chanson. E sempre la stessa canzone. Volver a la misma cancion.* Among the Tehuelche the songs are restricted to the mere repetition of completely meaningless sounds.[21] The text to the dancing songs of the Akrekuna consists in the eternally repeated word *Heia, heia.*[22]

Even when melodies are completely absent, there remains a vivid feeling for meter and rhythm. This can be observed among Negroes, whose melodic talents have been placed rather low by several writers.[23] Bowdich is surprised by the marvelous rhythmic control of the musicians throughout the multifarious complexity and disharmony of the music.[24] Schlagintwelt relates about the music in a Chinese Theater which was straining the listener's ears: "I was never able to find the melody. The beat, however, was kept strictly. It was communicated by the conductor through the forceful striking of two wooden sticks upon a board." [25] The same feeling of rhythm is mentioned of Melanesian peoples.

A speculative hypothesis is submitted here concerning the reason for the expression of emotions through rhythmic activities: When we are excited we seem to sense the beating of the heart and pulse more markedly because of the faster circulation of blood. Since these are markedly rhythmic, they tend in general towards rhythmic movements.

This drive toward rhythmic expression manifests itself sometimes in curious forms. Certain Australian tribes yield to it during songs when they pull the ends of their beards with their hands in keeping with the rhythms. (At least it seems to me that the passage in Browne concerning aboriginal Australians should be so understood.) [26] Arabic sailors mutually even hit their heads together when singing, which obviously occurs in rhythmically determined intervals.[27]

Therefore it is also true that we are least able to sing when we are in moods of depression or excitement, that is, whenever the heartbeat is very quiet or irregular. Then we are almost unable to stay with a rhythm which is in contrast to our inner oscillating feeling. A piano player who is afraid is the most likely to miss the beat. There is also a reciprocal effect. Whenever one is very much afraid and commences singing under great effort of will, the fear will be mitigated. Children will sing in darkness in order to rid themselves of fear. It has been observed that the beats of music even affect the heartbeat of man.[28] Quetelet found that his heartbeat accommodated itself to rhythmic motions which he heard or executed. It is then quite probable that, conversely, acoustical manifestations will be rhythmically structured by rhythmically felt pulses or heartbeats.[29]

When we are excited, we are not in a position to continue speaking in our usual manner. Our lungs, which work more diligently when we are excited, exhale air in a more intermittent fashion. Thus, the panting manner of speech is produced by certain excitements. Coughing, no doubt, contains an element of rhythm.[30] When a rhythmically and melodically formed linguistic sound has come into being, there may also have occurred a process analogous to that which was so important in the origin of language. There the memory of a sensation was closely connected with the memory of a sound which was instigated by it and perhaps produced simultaneously. When the emotion subsequently recurred, the repetition of the rhythmic or melodic sounds may have been all the more probable, easier and immediate.

IV

Let us now continue with questions concerning the origin of instrumental music. Similar at least to vocal music, which originated from mere speaking, it developed from mere noise. But it is much less a natural product, an unconscious emotional expression. Vischer has written extensively on the difference between vocal and instrumental music after their developments into art.[31] There he emphasizes that musical instruments "present resistance already as mere material matter." Hence, instrumental music can only reflect emotions that move man's moods, and not, as in songs, be a direct expression of the latter. This point of view, at least, cannot be tenable for the period of the origin of music.[32]

Whenever a tribesman on the war path yields to his inner emotions —which may also drive him to sing on this occasion—and clashes his weapons together resoundingly and rhythmically, could this act not be considered a direct expression of his emotion analogous to song? There are other emotions which lead to similar noises which could be called unintentional. Thus, the English doctor Chrichton Browne describes a female melancholic patient who spent hours rhythmically beating together the palms of her hands which were locked by her fingers. Why shouldn't the emotions which are able to induce the vocal chords to commence their special rhythmical movements which we call song and which lead the legs into the rhythmic movements of the dance, also induce the hands to their rhythmic clapping, which is the first and most natural beginning of instrumental music? And why shouldn't these emotions also induce the hands to use the instruments which may be at this moment in their grasp? The same considerations can be applied to the rhythmic stamping of the feet on the floor, and the noise which is thereby produced, which, in the same fashion as the clapping of hands, is a natural expression of emotions at the beginning of instrumental music. It is also a reason for the deep identity of music and dance. Among several very old national dances a special and important role is played by this stamping of the feet on the floor. Poeppig did not find any musical instrument amongst the Pehueuche. He only observed an identification of rhythm with the stamping of their feet whenever they sang and danced.[33] The simultaneous employment of both forms of musical expression all over the world, even on the lowest levels of musical development, can be explained by the identical source of instrumental and vocal music. This phenomenon otherwise is not at all intelligible. Their unification may also be based on the fact that excitements, reemphasized through singing, led to such rhythmical productions of noise, and thus, perhaps, to the most primitive form of accompaniment. In general, it is generally supposed that vocal music was the foundation of instrumental music. I cannot understand the rationale of this argument unless it is in the sense above. Among several Polynesian peoples the clapping of hands serves as the rhythmic accompaniment of singing in the place of instruments.[34] Brugsch relates the same of the Nubians.[35] It is reported of the northwest Caroline Islands that vocal music was accompanied there by beating out the rhythm on the waist.[36] Salvado writes: "Wind and stringed instruments are perfectly unknown among the natives of Nuaova Norcia, as are also unknown to them any variety of drums. They accompany their singing, however, by the joyous striking together of their weapons." [37]

Stringed instruments are less widely distributed than wind instruments. The construction and principle of stringed instruments point away from a period of musical development in which music was primarily a product of simple psycho-physical causes, and not of artistic intentions. Flutes belong more to the period of nature. This is because of their origin as well as of their effects and technical conditions. Stringed instruments belong more to the period of art. Even highly developed antiquity did not transcend a quite inadequate harp in the area of string instruments.[38]

This immediate effect of wind instruments accounts for their almost exclusive use in conjunction with mere noise instruments for the purposes of mystic and exciting occasions. The South African magician (*Mganga*), uses a magic horn; the music of horns and flutes surrounds the orgiastic cults of Cybele and Dionysus. The music for the Buddhist service in Tibet is executed with wind instruments and drums.[39]

For the same reason, primitive people have a vivid feeling for wind instruments. Rhythms can be more sharply characterized by them and they approximate vocal music—probably the first form of music—more closely than string instruments. "Lartet has described two flutes, made out of the bones and horns of the reindeer, found in caves together with flint tools and the remains of extinct animals." [40]

Martins relates how he did not at all impress the Indians with his violin playing. Very soft flutes also do not seem to impress various primitive peoples greatly, as Seeman tells us about the Eskimo of the Pacific Ocean.[41] Other peoples enjoy these and especially loud instruments more. When the Magyars came to Western Europe they only knew wind instruments, since only the words which designate these are of national origin. Those for the other instruments are taken over from European languages. This tendency was maintained through the days of Ladislaus VI and Ludwig II. From the rank order which existed in their times one can see that the musicians of wind instruments had a higher rank over others in the royal orchestras.[42] This, perhaps, corresponds with the more emotional and warlike character of this nation. Even today our own military music is predominantly noise and wind music, and certainly not only because of technical reasons. The Kamchatka people also developed only clarinet-like wind instruments.[43] In Lithuania and Estonia the bagpipe is the oldest and most widely spread instrument.[44] Polynesians [45] only know the drum, flute, and shell trumpet, as do the Melanesians [46] and the old Mexicans.[47]

There is an approximate analogy between the developments of vocal and instrumental music. Mere noise, the beginning of the latter, corresponds to the sound of the words which form the beginning of the former. Rhythmically organized language, which is the decisive step towards vocal music, corresponds to the rhythmic production of noise and to those wind instruments which only produce a few monotonously alternating notes. Finally, the melodic variation of pitch, genuine singing which follows rhythms and is not as shown by our development a purely natural product, corresponds to those instruments which melodically alternate several tones.

The earliest instruments that can be found are therefore noise instruments. Bossmann tells us that the Moors had at least ten different drums.[48] He felt their music to be intensely barbaric. Among the most ancient Greek instruments we find manifold forms of noise instruments: sistron, tympanon, chrotaion, chumbalon. Among Indians, Waitz only sees noise instruments, rarely a flute with a maximum of six holes. Freycinet praises the 'very melodic airs' of the music of the Timor; of instruments, however, they only knew the little drum, the big drum, and other noise instruments.[49] The noise instrument of the slaves of Rio de Janeiro, which is described by Wilkes,[50] is distributed around the whole world. It is a rattle "made of tin similar to a child's rattle." Every ethnological museum shows the immense distribution of this instrument which appears in a great number of variations. Frequently it is made of dried and hollowed-out fruits which are filled with seeds or pebbles.[51]

V

Monotony is predominant in the vocal as well as instrumental music of primitive peoples. It is derived from the origin of music in non-melodic noise. This is so even in areas where the means are available for more melodic presentations and on occasions on which we would tend to expect a more sensually appealing form of music.[52] Quaas describes the music which accompanies the most seductive dances of the Bajaderes as being most monotonous and played on flutes and drums.[53] "When a Chinese expects success of his show of dedication when serenading, he will have to repeat his song for several hours. A three-to-hour-hundred-fold repetition is not rare, since Chinese love songs seldom contain more than four stanzas.[54] Tylor tells of Mexican dances which he observed in Coroyotta: "A man and a woman stood facing each other, an old man tinkled the guitar producing a strange, endless, monotonous tune, and the two dancers stamped their feet and moved their arms and bodies about in time to the music, throwing themselves into affected and voluptuous attitudes. . . ."[55] Whoever has attended a performance of a Tarantella near the Gulf of Naples will have observed to what feverish extent such monotonous music is able to stimulate the blood, and how far it can be adapted to sensual and voluptuous dances. Monotonous music also increases mystical excitement. This may be the reason for the monotony of songs that are connected with religious exercises, no less in the litanies of Christian and Judaic churches than in the religious ceremonies of African and Asiatic peoples.[56]

VI

As language relates to concrete thought, so music does to diffuse emotional feelings. The first creates the second, because the second creates the first. Similarly, in poetry, the imagination of the poet kindles an analogous one in the listener. In the case of music, perceptual imaginations are replaced by far less defined emotions. In poetry these occur only intermediately. Among poets, the feelings precede the imaginations, while among listeners they follow them.

The assumption that music stimulates the emotions which precede the creative work of poets makes situations like the following easy to understand. Before writing poetry, Alfieri usually prepared himself mentally by listening to music. He once remarked, "almost all my tragedies were sketched in my mind while I listened to music or within a few hours thereafter." Milton was filled with solemn inspiration while he listened to the sound of an organ. For the sensitive poet Warburton, too, music was a necessity. A famous French preacher, Massillon, drafted the outline of his sermons which he had to deliver to the court, while he played his violin. Drawing on Streicher, Palleske refers to the stimulation which Schiller reputedly derived from music. The ancient custom of musical preludes before rhapsodies is likely related to this. Today the custom is preserved by composers who usually begin a song with a prelude of the accompanying instruments rather than with the immediate singing.

In order to understand properly the specific psychological characteristics of music, we cannot place enough stress on the transitional process from the affects and emotions of the performer through his music to the feelings and sensations of the listener. This process is cognitively understood much less for music than for any other art form. The superficial rationalistic conception of the eighteenth century's psychological research is characteristically represented by Euler, who writes: "The enjoyment of music derives from one's ability to guess correctly the intentions and emotions of the composer, the execution of which will fill one's soul with a comfortable satisfaction if one considers the composition a fortunate one." [57]

The enjoyment of music as art is contrasted with these relatively emotional patterns on the basis of only quantitative and not at all qualitative dimensions. Contemporary as compared with very primitive music produces such a myriad of feelings of great variety that an equilibrium ensues among them through their restraining relationships on one another. The result then is objectivity. Helmholtz writes:

It would be important to discover whether the significant and highly varied expression of emotions which is produced by music cannot be derived from the very same form of emotional activity which is responsible for the movement of (bodily) limbs, just as the variations of the pitch level in song is caused by innervations of muscles. The recurrence of the sequence of physical-psychical phenomena of which we spoke here and earlier explains many effects of music. If, indeed, as I suppose, musical expressions are influenced by the rhythm of excited heartbeats, then it is natural that musical expression will be produced for the listener by the latter. This will be the result of physiological connections as well as of psychic associations and reproduction.[58]

VII

During the course of its development, music rejects its natural characteristics more and more.[59] The further it advances, the closer it approximates the ideal of art. Through this process it approaches objectivity, which is the highest honor for the (performing) artist. This does not mean that all feelings, or only the very climatic and sanguine ones, disappear from music, nor that they should not become excited by it or should no longer excite themselves. It means only that music and its manner of presentation should not be the immediate result of these emotions, as it was originally; but instead, that it should become an image of them, which is reflected in the mirror of beauty. It is in this sense that the old explanation should be understood, according to which music, or any other art, is supposed to be imitation. Music imitates the tones which spring forth from the soul when elicited by a strong emotion. Above all this seems to me to be the decisive point in the explanation of music as an art form. Naturally it refers also to instrumental music, which in a very crude and initial approximation of art imitates those reflex-like rhythmic noises.

Even though the first production of musical sounds is originally accompanied by words, they can be omitted. Intense emotions produce the tones, and it is the latter, of course, which are important. I have observed singers who did not pay proper attention to the texts of their songs, and who thus sang all imaginable forms of contradictory meanings. Nevertheless, they performed the melodies with the truest and deepest emotional expression and comprehension. This is a perfect proof of the artistic character of music: music produces typical sensations which include completely the more individual sensations produced by words.

With deep insight, language refers to the making of music as "play" or "playing." Nowadays music is indeed play, and must be such if it is to be art. But in its inception music was serious to the same degree as speech and exclamation and all other natural sounds.

VIII

Victor Renauld, the French engineer, sees it as significant that it is almost exclusively the women who create new verbal expressions as well as songs and dirges among the Botucotu peoples. In Siam music is almost the single occupation of women: "The highest ambition of the fair sex in Siam is to possess the faculty of performing the graceful evocations and charming tunes of the *Lakhon-pu-Yng*. Their perception of concord in notes is as acute as that of European musicians and they are equally as long in tuning their instruments."[60] According to Andree,[61] women are the poets and composers among the Kamchatka. In Estonia only women are assigned to singing.[62] With the exception of two women, there is no mention of lyrical or sung poetry in the Old Testament from the times of Moses to David. These are Deborah, who sings her song of victory (even though she sings with Barak),[63] and Hannah, who sings her song of praise on the occasion of Samuel's birth.[64] Delaborde writes about the Hungarian Magyars: "One sees again, among the peasant farmers who maintain primitive customs for extended times, that the younger girls assemble on holidays and join in singing together odes and ancient poetry. Never are they accompanied by young men."[65] On the Fiji Islands it is only the women and children who sing. Men of the higher ranks never sing.[66]

It is remarkable that the close association between dance and music becomes reversed among some people as soon as the question of prestige enters into consideration. Among the Romans, vocal music was despised even during very early times. Dancing was even considered a vice. However, already during the period of Gracchus, young boys of noble descent were taught to sing.[67] For many years to come, the dance was treated as a sign of the most reprehensible lack of good taste. According to Vambery, the Oesbeges consider as decent only the dance of women. Musical instruction is given, however, to the princes of the house of the lord.[68] Sexual differentiation of activities is also attested by the opposite fact: among the Tehuelche, it is the men who dance,[69] as they do in Turkey, where other reasons, however, may be the cause. In Hisiuen, Gatteron found a strict separation between men and women during their very obscene dances.[70] Chamisso reports that on Radak the women sing all the songs which deal with war and navigation.[71] Among the Mede, music was also primarily in the hands of women.[72] According to Busch, it appears that only women played a certain horn among the Negroes of the Mississippi.[73]

Australian men are led to the most sensual actions by the songs of their women.[74] The women of Madagascar even believed that their singing and dancing at home would invigorate the daring, courage, and energy of their husbands away at war.[75] A contradictory argument should also be cited here: Pirschewalski observes that the women seem to be less musical among the Mongols than their men.[76] At the same time, he reports, their position towards men is absolutely inferior. This effect probably corresponds to the emotional expression which we examined above.

Animals, at least, can be induced through music to engage in sexual relations.[77] Among musical insects it is only the females who make music.

When, during their lascivious festivities, after some mere singing, the Kimbande women dance the reprehensible Kanye dance and permit their men, who would like to stimulate them to further possible excesses, to join, they add drumming and flute playing.[78] Sirens seduced travelers through their songs. "Don't get familiar with the singing girl so that she doesn't catch you through her charm." [79] It is not decent for a single man to sing or dance among Persians despite their passionate love for music and dancing. Only low-caste people practiced music which was not connected with religious services.[80] "The lips of the whore are sweeter than honeydew and her voice is smoother than oil."[81]

Relationships between music and sexual processes can be demonstrated among all primitive peoples who use the puberty and circumcision ceremonies of young men and girls as cause for festivities at which they employ music in a major role.[82]

Since women are more actively engaged in producing music, it is quite conceivable that their receptivity to music is also stronger. Dobritzhofer writes that he was immediately able to attract a crowd of females through his violin playing, but, only later, crowds of young men.[83] Salvado relates of the songs of the Australian aborigines: "Songs of lamentation afflict their facial expressions in a mask-like manner, and especially so for the women who are truly full of tears." [84] Ethnographic observations show that the differentiation of the sexes was recognized early by primitive peoples and probably led to mystical meanings and commands. Among the Ashanti, no woman is ever permitted to touch any of the numerous musical instruments. She is permitted only to participate in singing.[85] There is a variety of Indian songs which may only be sung by men.[86] On Lukanor there are songs which are only to be sung by women and others which are only permitted to men.[87] In Loango music is performed in huts which are inhabited by girls during their first menstrual period. This music is produced on the primitive instruments which are restricted for use by females: the *ntubu* and the *kuimbi*. These have to be available in each virgin's hut.[88]

IX

Undoubtedly the true nature of music is revealed, even more clearly than in previous examples, in refrain singing, which at first sight could be treated as a pure mode of artistic expression. The origin of this form of expression, however, can only have been the excitement of an audience which resulted from the singing of a single individual. They must have joined the singing unconsciously—at first probably not to the same melody, but in a wild mixture of tones. This style of singing is still purely subjective. The circumstances of this first group singing are without significance. What matters is only the emotional impact which results from it. But this could have been caused equally well by some other event. Only after a feeling of objectivity has been established, and a certain sense for harmonious sound developed, can people join in the melody of a song by which they were stimulated. Even today, when we are excited by some musical composition, we will sing along, partly or even completely unaware of it; at least we might move our hands or feet in the appropriate rhythm. Whenever primitive people sing simple refrains there occurs a combination of natural and artistic elements. The mood which is created by the song leader induces the audience to sing. When they sing the same tones as he does, and repeat his tones, this turns into a kind of imitation which approaches art. Even here a purely natural force is engaged. The first song might have stimulated related feelings in the audience. These, in turn, might lead to a corresponding, even though not identical, song. After some repetition of this process, one could anticipate the climactic point of the effects at which one would be induced most strongly to join in the singing—at least of already familiar tunes. This means of course that the effect would occur with certainty.

Most American Indian songs have refrains which are sung by a chorus.[89] Freycinet tells about his experiences on the island of Timor: the person who leads the dancers, sings the words; the refrain is repeated by the choir.[90] Winwood Reade states that whenever the African Negro is excited he will start singing, another one will answer with a song, while the rest of the company will mumur a chorus in complete unison as if touched by a musical wave.[91] Brugsch reports, concerning a song melody of his sailors from Nubia: "One sings a solo while the choir accompanies his song by the clapping of hands and repeats selected parts." [92] The recitation of the classical Greek Chorus was sung, and the selected melodies were so simple and popular with the audiences that they sometimes joined in those tunes which were known to them.[93] Pontécoulant reports that Negroes frequently sing during the sugar cane harvest in order to overcome fatigue. They do this in the following manner: a female Negro with a sonorous voice commences singing a couplet, then the refrain is repeated by the chorus.[94] Pindar writes that the people at the Olympic festivals repeated the refrain *Tenella Challiniche* three times after the announcement of the name of the victor. This is an ancient custom.[95]

X

At the same point begins the development of the folk song. When one understands, on theoretical and empirical grounds, how especially pleasing passages of solo singers invite the audience to join and repeat the music, then it follows that those songs will have become more popular which contain many of such pleasing passages. They will thus have been remembered more easily. The lyrical connection further facilitates the memorizing of these tunes. It is quite likely that the individual members of a tribe will have progressed from the original imitative group singing to solo singing whenever they felt like singing in those tunes which were now familiar to them.

There seems to be a strong tendency among human beings in general to express one's mood through already familiar melodies before the exploration of new ones.[96] These songs, which were first sung by a single individual, and which became popular through the imitation of refrain-like passages, probably instigated others to join in the singing, because they corresponded most with the characteristics of the audience. It is on this basis that they have spread. Whenever the characteristics of a people tend toward extremes, the more emotional melodies first invite others to join in the singing; if they are of a more sombre nature, the more melancholic melodies lead to the independent expressions of these moods. Eventually, it will invite the repetition of the music for the simple delight in doing so.[97] Just as it is likely that the expressions of the more talented individuals have found a wider acceptance during the developmental process of language, so it is quite likely that the vocal songs of the more important tribesmen will be imitated more readily. This is on account of their improved expression of sensations and their views or perceptions of the other members of society—and because people will have listened to them more attentively and employed their verbal practices more frequently.

Among savages whose points of view are quite restricted, he who knows how to express a quality of the people's soul with a more developed degree of perfection than the average tribesman will be considered of importance. Usually secular or priestly powers are connected with inspirational performances. It is likely that tribesmen could be especially attentive to the expression of the individual who is distinguished in this fashion. On this basis the wide distribution of vocal music can also be explained, because these songs represent the content of the people's living spirit.

This very basic quality of music, the ability to represent the people's soul, is found to an especially perfected degree within single individuals who are supported by talent or genius. A man will have these qualities basically because he is a product of his people, whose total self was formed through life within the society. His personal gifts could only reinforce the received stimuli. To speak in an analogy, it is as if these personal qualities had been invested for higher rates of return than they would have been by the wide mass of the people. The more highly gifted individual's melodies will be spread among the people and turned into folk song in the manner which we already described. Just as one can truthfully say about the oratory of a popular representative, who was elected by the total society because of his ability to represent most intensely and accurately the individualities of the nation, that he only pronounces the words which the people have spoken, so, applying the same logic in accordance with our previous discussion, we are indeed entitled to consider these individual melodies as emanations of the folk soul.[98] In this case the usually more individualized representations of the folk soul were intensified in the focal point of the talents of some individuals.

XI

In addition to the expression of general emotions in folk song, there is another especially significant phenomenon. It is found especially on the lower levels of musical practice: music is sometimes used for the expression of very specialized and concrete images. Dallas writes: "It is very remarkable, that the Maroons had a particular call upon the horn for each individual, by which he was summoned from a distance as easily as he could have been addressed by name had he been near." [99] Bowdich observes: "The natives in Ashanti maintain that they are able to converse amongst one another by playing the flute. An older resident of Akkra assured me that he had listened to such conversations, and that every sentence had been explained to him. All Chieftains in Ashanti have special melodies for their horns." [100] In Tyrolean society yodeling is frequently employed for purposes of communication. The same can be said for the songs of Venetian gondoliers and the women of the Lido. American Indians have special melodies for the designation of the seasons.[101] In Persia a certain tonality, *Zer-keki*, produces images of wealth.[102] In the Cameroons the news is spread by the sounding of horns, and royal orders are publicized in the same fashion on Bissaux.[103] On Tahiti the same phenomenon occurs, when there are certain songs for the construction of houses, others for cutting down trees or the launching of boats in the ocean.[104] There is a special melody which is employed for the ancient bridal dance between the bride and the pastor in Soedermann-land.[105] From Wildheufluhen near Klosters it has been reported that the meaning of the first excited shout to be heard on St. Jacob's Day is that the respective shepherd has taken possession of a maid.[106] On the Fiji Island the people are called together for cannibalistic festivals by a special drum beat which is only used for this occasion.[107] That there exists some form of relationship between the factors of personality and the forms of musical expression finds its utterance in the familiar proverb that comes to us from the German: "Whose bread I eat, whose song I sing."

XII

Since music is originally a natural resultant of emotional excitement, and since listening to it can only produce excitement, it would seem to be a contradiction that, especially as emphasized by the Greeks, music should also evoke quieting and calming responses. The resolution lies in the following argument: The effects of music are indirect. Indeed, the only way music can act on man is in the form of stimuli. But when the response it generates is in the direction opposite to the previously existing emotion, it will weaken that emotion. That is why one may put people to sleep through singing.[108] As we have shown above, music may bring with it a rise of the life spirit through its stimulation of joyful and mystical sensations. There is nothing more natural than that especially painful emotions will be weakened by this contrasting process.

Only as a fully developed art, devoid of direct reciprocity between the sensations of the performers and listeners, can music produce a weakening of emotions in the listeners. On the same basis, however, this force could not have originated in the performers.

Plato mentions the melancholic mood of musicians: Greek music[109] had its major purpose in the mentioned weakening of emotional states. It is possible that the nature of musicians was gradually influenced by the effects which they aimed for and produced. It is further possible that external equanimity may be observable even while very strong artistic emotions are at work.[110]

XIII

Salvado reports about the Australian aborigines: "Many times in their undulating dancing songs I saw them encouraged and stimulated in their labor in the fields. Not once, but many times they fell to the ground depleted of their strength and vigor. But, then they began to sing 'Machielo, Machiele,' which was one of their best known and favorite songs." [111] Then they commenced to sing and dance by themselves and then to return with new courage and vigor to their work. Thus, music is used everywhere for the relief of workers. [112]

Freycinet writes about Timor: "When the inhabitants work, they sing almost without stopping, especially if the occupation they are engaging in, needs the cooperation of many individuals and a sort of simultaneousness of action, such as having to paddle in a *piroque* (Pit pan), carry heavy loads jointly, thresh the rice . . . and to encourage one another to work." [113]

Quintilian writes: "Nor is this function of music confined to cases where the efforts of a number are given union by the sound of some sweet voice that sets the tune, but even solitary workers find solace at their toil in artless songs." [114] There are also some animals—for example camels during their fatiguing trips across the desert—which through music are invigorated to renewed efforts.

It is also known from passages in the writings of Plutarch, Pollux, and Aristotle that ancient peoples whipped their slaves to the accompaniment of music so as to make their punishment more tolerable. According to Waitz, the Eskimo eased over the most miserable situations by making music and dancing. [115] From Egyptian reliefs we learn that during the immense slave labor which was employed for the moving of monoliths, a man was standing high upon a stone in order to sing and mark a rhythm with his hands. The same custom in the most recent times is still frequently observed in this region even though, of course, under quite different conditions. Hammer, for example, reports this in a review of Villoteau. [116]

Most unusual effects of music, especially upon Negroes, are known from several different descriptions. [117] No doubt the fanaticism of Shamans, of the cult of Cybele, and of similar phenomena is largely the result of the music which is employed during those occasions. Such orgies naturally disappear among the more advanced peoples.

Nevertheless, many exciting effects remained through classical antiquity, as is illustrated by previously mentioned examples. The Spartan revolution was suppressed by Terpander through the powers of music. Well known is the political importance which was accorded music in the classical Greek state. Plato says of Damon that it would be impossible to change his music without changing the constiutional order of the state. The extended passage in Volume III of Plato's *Republic* must be mentioned, in which he examines the influence of tonality, rhythm, and instruments upon the emotional make-up. Accordingly he permits or prohibits forms of music in the structure of the state. To Plato music is only an educational tool.

The censors in Rome disapproved of all musical instruments in the year 639. An exception was made for the simple flute. The alleged influence on morals of flutes and string instruments were characteristically reversed in Rome and Greece. Greek political leaders were more dedicated to cultivate the Greek soul in a calm manner, while the Romans preferred characters as energetic and excited as possible, in correspondence with the warlike tendencies of the Roman state.

XIV

To several observers it has appeared remarkable that primitive people should prefer very monotonous music, yet depict fantastic, adventurous, loudly colored, and abnormal figures in their pictorial endeavors. Thus it was shown among the Botocudo. Martius observes of them, and of all other original inhabitants of America who employ extremely monotonous musical forms: "He (the original inhabitant of America) is able to exaggerate the unusual, the grotesque and the untamed into colossal forms, and to depict the scarce item in immense and horrible expressions." The people of the Fiji Islands similarly love most the cruel, exciting and fantastic horror stories while their music is abominably monotonous. First, these people are much closer to the origin of music in language. Since music originated and developed only through the gradual exaggeration of modulation and rhythm, it must have been quite monotonous initially. The original organic connection between music and linguistic usage was a limiting factor, which can still be observed in the modern recitative.

Some monotony is nevertheless dominant in the pictorial art of primitive people. Humboldt writes that primitive people are driven by their spiritual talents to the simplification and generalization of contours, and to the rhythmic repetition and serialization of pictures. Hence a tendency to monotonously rhythmical expression can be contrasted with a tendency to fantastic expressions. A distinct aspect of this imitative drive of uncivilized peoples can also be observed today in the tendency of lower-class people to copy identical emblems or signs on a rock or tree which has previously been so marked by a passerby.[118] We have evidence for this from petroglyphs from all over the world. The best description can be found in Andree. For the sake of analogy, however, compare also page 121 (of the original essay).

Despite the monotony of primitive songs, there is nevertheless a stark disharmonic concord of many voices and a similarity of structure of the individual tonal sequences. Baker maintains that since the Arabs' stomachs prefer raw meat and the still smoking liver instantaneously extracted from a killed animal, so their ears prefer, in similar fashion, rough and disharmonic music.[119] On this basis we can construct an analogy, even though I do not wish to pretend that it is a perfect one: to the same extent to which monotonously repetitive pictures consist in individually and fantastically formed wild images, so monotonous songs consist in the repetition of disharmonically shrill individual tones or sounds.

We know that Indians and Arabs possess, in contrast to their apparently unmusical development, a sharp unbelievably developed sense of hearing. They are able to hear over distances which would silence all noises for European ears. There is a relevant passage in Steinthal's *Der Ursprung der Sprache*: "I derived the advancement of man over the animals almost completely from his erect posture." In addition there are to be considered the other senses, except for the tactile sense. One is here reminded of Herder. All these senses are weaker in their extensive effects, but stronger intensively, that is, they are able to receive more impressions which are spread over shorter distances. Consequently, a greater variety of individual qualities is discovered in things and similar appearances of various phenomena are more exactly differentiated.[120]

I would like to point out that the sharpness of hearing of the more primitive peoples is formed only because of the necessities of life. These people are dependent upon this sense for the discovery both of food and of their enemies. It may also stem from the continuous quietude which surrounds most primitive peoples. Their acute sense of vision may be derived from the limitless horizon. People who live within narrow walls tend to become short-sighted. On account of these conditions one may advance the hypothesis that the development of their senses is quite one-sided, since it is aimed at the perception of very soft sounds or vibrations of extremely low intensity. The ability to analyze complex vibrations, which occur during the simultaneous sounding of different tones, into their acoustical components, does not necessarily go with this. If this were so, then it would be a most interesting observation with relevance to Fechner and especially to Erhard's *Otiatrik* which is cited there.[121] That the development of the acoustical sense is a partial process which is not necessarily connected with musical growth, is attested by G. Carus, who describes Wilhelm von Humboldt as an "acoustical man," though he obviously was scarcely receptive to music.[122]

XV

The invention of musical themes for Greek melodies was restricted by the limited number of tones available on the stringed instruments. The charm and stimulation of this music could not, therefore, be based on the thematic constructions and novelty, but had rather to be found in the refinement and nuances of their performances. This is similar to Greek dramatic productions, which strove for perfect execution and variety within a frequently repeated dramatic plot and content. Schopenhauer remarks that the greater an artistic creation is, the less it owes its greatness to plot and content.

Polyphonic music marks the conclusion of the development of music towards art. Now it was in need of complicated rules. As was already noted, there were beginnings in this direction over extended periods of time. Nothing originated, however, which would resemble our own music. Hucbald (who died in 930 A.D.) made the first known attempt to connect several voices harmonically. He found it aesthetically pleasing to have parallel sixths and fourths proceed in musical sequences! Rousseau also desired to return to the simplicity of pure nature in music. Thus he devalued all polyphonic music. In an erroneous manner he frequently found the means for the fulfillment of his ideals in extrinsic or superficial aspects.[123] In consideration of the Greeks, he composed an air of only four tones. Tartini entertained similar ideas.

In the more highly educated social circles, interest in music was created which had previously not been present. At the same time, the music of lower social strata lost more and more. Here I remind the reader of the phenomenon of the Meistersinger, who attempted to raise folk music to higher and more artistic perfection. But they succeeded only in creating confused artificial calculations similar to Gothic structures. The warmth of life was missing in their art, which lacked the sunshine of personal genius.

Nevertheless, it is erroneous to believe that the nation is without influence upon musical developments. Probably nobody has any doubt concerning the developments in the other arts which have to be national if they are to reach and maintain the blossom of perfection. This does not at all mean that they have to be patriotic. Indeed, history even shows that the arts could produce the most beautiful examples in the most politically disorganized states—analogous to blooming flowers on the top of a rubbish heap. I wish simply to convey this: whatever great and well-developed talents an individual may bring into his life, only the life of his home country, which surrounds him from his very first day, will make him into what he is. It will form his character in him. It gives him his ends, and his means to them. The greater his talents are, the more he will accept from the material which is available to him in the national cultural heritage. This will take place without his specific action, without his becoming conscious of it during the years of his growth.

If an artist is to maintain a uniform style of work—without which it is impossible to become a great artist—he will not change the character of his drives as he receives them through the nature and culture of his society. He will have to guard his style, not because it is patriotic, not because it would be unpatriotic for a German to work in French mannerisms, but for the simple reason that his psycho-tendencies and the moral nature which he gained by his upbringing in his society form the best foundation for his form of art or style of creation. If he were to imitate models which are different from the national style, he would fracture his essence, and his art would decline. In this sense, then, he has to work on the basis of his national background and historical foundation. He does not necessarily have to be conscious of this, nor does he have to have nationalistic feelings.

It is not yet possible to state verbally the national differences in music, since the psychological dimension of music has not been adequately examined. If one considers the total development of the last 150 years of German music and compares it with the French and Italian, there can be no doubt that each is quite different, and not interchangeable with the others, either in character or in individual compositions. Obviously we cannot prove conclusively why a particular form of music necessarily had to be created by the particular characteristics of a people. The differentiation of music into national forms nevertheless demonstrates that such effects must take place. Further, just as even the most subjective and individualistic poetic product is, to a large extent, indebted to the linguistic usage of the national language in which it is written—there is a saying that it "imagines and thinks for everybody"—so there is an historically developed folk music present for everybody else. By folk music, of course, I do not mean only folk songs, that is, the type of music which the folk creates for its own consumption, but I include in the term all forms of the national musical literature.

The history of music shows in almost every case that a composer bases his creations on the precepts of his precursors. This implies that the sum of the historical musical development of a society forms the foundation of his musical culture. The composer, therefore, owes so much to the chain of his precursors that he would never have become what he is without them.[124] Of course, his musical taste is formed from his earlieset day by continuous listening to the previously created national musical heritage. The frequent chance to listen to a given music would not be available—and in modern times one is almost continuously surrounded by it—if this music did not correspond completely with the culture of a people, and if it were not fully accepted by them. Thus the composer receives through tradition the music which directs his work.[125] This is similar to the poet who transforms through his own works the language of his people which is given to him.

In accordance with this line of argument, the foundations on which every composer has to build are of national character. We may further consider the influence which is exercised upon an artist who notices that a certain composition of an earlier composer is enthusiastically received by his people while another is neglected. Thus, if one considers the complete historical development of music, it is impossible to assume that musical history occurs independently of other national events as a sort of state within a state. We maintain this even though we have not yet discovered the formal relationship between the musical and other contents of the people's soul.

XVI

In the early state of natural man, when nationalistic feelings are not yet developed, we find the same musical phenomena all over the world. We find similar musical instruments and melodies, the same emotional creation of music, and a dedication to the production of nerve-shattering effects. Later on, however, nationalistic elements become more and more observable. We see, for example, that Asiatic instruments were abhorred during the period of Greece's highest development. The same fate was accorded the Greek instruments during the time of Rome's strongest national consciousness. We observe also the characteristic contrast between the French and German manner of violin playing which is maintained in a way which could almost be described as being governed by jealousy. Moreover, a certain style of international music, in which several composers worked during the nineteenth century (Liszt, Berlioz), does not seem to prosper. This happens because their music is not properly rooted in any soil. How vehement national contrasts can become in music is illustrated, for example, by occurrences in Paris which are reported in the article on Lully in the *Biographie Universelle*.

Jean Jacques Rousseau placed himself on the front line (of the partisans of Italian music). His letter "On French Music" became the signal for a war of opinions which was responsible for a considerable number of brochures. In the parterre of the Opera House the public was divided in two camps which ranged from the one side of the loge of the king to the side of the queen's loge. The corner of the king contained the defenders of French music; the admirers of Italian music were in the queen's corner. The parties abused one another to the point that they almost turned to fist fighting.

This is reminiscent of the Circus Parties in classical Rome. There, the same interesting process can be observed in which the initial objective of the fight becomes fully unimportant. The significance of the initial objective then turns into an excuse for the excesses of the fighters. In music, however, this phenomenon occurs much more frequently than in other arts and sciences, since more believe themselves to be competent to participate here. Every fight which involves greater numbers also increases in violence. The less one can reasonably fight verbally about music, the more frequent these fights become. One can observe frequently how deaf mutes and other sick people, who for some other reason cannot speak, turn into a state of exaggeration which is frightening and out of all proportion whenever one does not understand their hand signs. Without comparing these phenomena any further, I would suggest that their psychological causes are quite related. It is impossible to express adequately through words the concrete bases of one's opinions concerning music. Our language does not have expressions for such sensations. Thus individuals cannot understand one another. Understanding is even less likely when one man has always had an opinion which the other cannot understand. This failure of communication feeds the violence which occurs frequently over aesthetic and especially musical controversies.

Amiot played for some Chinese, who themselves were completely enraptured by their own music, "the most beautiful sonatas, the most melodious and brilliant flute melodies." The only effect was that he tortured and bored them with his playing. They told him that "these melodies were not for our ears and that our ears were not for these melodies." The miraculous power of the national elements in music is also attested to by the following account which I borrow from a journal:

When Bonaparte was in Egypt he attempted by all means at his disposal, by all miracles of occidental science, to influence the Moslems and to gain their sympathy. On the advice of Monge he also experimented with music. One evening a large orchestra of the most highly skilled musicians was assembled on the Esbekieh Place in Cairo. Now, in the presence of the country's most noble people and a large audience a whole series of musical compositions was performed. There were serious compositions, learned music, some simple, some soft melodies, military marches and rousing fanfares. All efforts were in vain! The Moslems remained unmoved and full of composure during the whole procedure, just like the mummies in their catacombs. Monge was beside himself. "Those blockheads don't deserve that you exercise yourself anymore," he shouted to the musicians. "Play them Marlbrough. Perhaps that will suit them!"

> Marlbrough s'en va-t-en guerre,
> Mirliton, Mirliton ton taine,
> Marlbrough s'en va-t-en guerre,
> Ne sait quand reviendra!

The orchestra began to play and a sort of miracle happened. Already with the first tones, thousands of the mummified faces showed signs of life. There was a happy motion which spread through the crowd of listeners. For a moment one could believe that all the serious Moslems, old and young, would rush into the open streets and commence to dance. This little song made them so happy. From now on Marlbrough was played every evening, and every night the result was the same.

How can one possibly explain this remarkable occurrence? Gretry, Haydn, Mozart do not leave any impression, while the Marlbrough song happily excites all the people. Chateaubriand believed that he could explain this strange phenomenon. For he mentions that the origin of the melody of the Marlbrough song is Arabic. The song itself belongs in the Middle Ages and was most probably brought to Spain by the Knights of the Cross during the reign of Don Jayme I (1213–1276) of Aragon, and brought to France during the reign of Louis IX (1226–1270). The song tells the story of the knight Mambron, a participant in the holy war of whom nothing else is known. This story in music and word formed the little song which was used by Madame Poitrine in order to bring to sleep her royal suckling who was the son of Louis XVI. Queen Marie Antoinette accidentally overheard the little song. She liked it, imitated it, and through her it became so fashionable that it soon was heard all over Europe. Through a ridiculous accident, the name of the Duke of Marlborough, or Marlbrough (John Churchill), the victor of Malplaquet, replaced that of the Knight of the Cross, Sire Mambron. Thus, the Moslems in Egypt heard in this melody the sound of an old national tune and were moved thereby.

Bodenstedt describes the national music of Persia as ear-shattering. He tells of young Asiatics who were raised and educated in St. Petersburg, but who enjoyed the small and big drum beats of their native Asiatic musicians on their occasional visits to their home country much more than all the musical highlights that were presented to them at the St. Petersburg Concerts.[126] The very same observation is made by Polak.[127]

One should finally consider that music is not only expressive of the character of a population, but that it is also influenced by the cyclical movements of the people's history which raises and lowers it. Ambros points out in the preface to the *Geschichte der Musik*, Vol. 2, that every rise in the cultural life also provides a new impetus for musical developments.[128]

XVII

Because of its characteristics, yodeling seems to belong among the most primitive forms of musical expression. Essentially it is, however, so different from song that the discussion of the origin of vocal music does not cover it properly. Since it is impossible for an individual to gather by himself the necessary experience for the explanation of this phenomenon, I published in the *Jahrbuch des Schweizer Alpenclub, Jahrgang 1879*, a series of questions concerning the nature of yodeling which were also included in other journals. The result was a number of answers from authorities on Alpine living.[129] Unfortunately they contained so many contradictions that one must conclude that yodeling is characteristically different in various Alpine regions.

The following inductive results were drawn together by me from the common elements of these reports and my own observations: Yodeling consists in a rather short series of tones, which are produced without verbal connection, on the bases of only single letters which are almost exclusively vowels. Characteristically there is a continuous interchange between the chest and head register while omitting the falsetto. Each so-called breaking of the speaking voice, which may be the result of emotional strain or other strenuous exertions, illustrates the protoplasm of yodeling. If now one considers that a relatively loud speaking or shouting voice is almost continuously required for the purposes of communication in mountainous regions, then yodeling might originally have been nothing more than a shout which is shifted into the head register. In particular the exertion of the lungs from the continuous rise in altitude seems to dispose the voice to this abrupt shift. Both conditions are found together exclusively in higher mountain regions where yodeling, too, is almost exclusively observed. The frequent recurrence of yodeling may have been the cause for its development into an artistic style. Additional support for the hypothesis concerning the analogous relationship between yodeling and shouting is to be found in the fact that frequently yodeling is added at the conclusion of a song where other people add more or less articulated shouts.

We wish now to turn our attention to the view of Jaeger, already mentioned in Section I of this essay. According to him, yodeling is the origin of song; it is stimulated by the sexual drive, and becomes the vehicle for its fulfillment. I do not wish to deny that his shifting of the vocal registers might possibly occur when the sexual drive is expressed through shouting. However, there is no foundation for a causal nexus between the latter and the former. Moreover, yodeling is observed only among Alpine populations, and is employed with preference in the age group of eight to fourteen years, when one can hardly speak of sexual fulfillment.[130] A final observation should be added. Yodeling indeed is not the characteristic means of communication between boys and girls. The majority of the replies to my questions emphatically deny any such relationship. Only a single one from St. Gailen mentions that yodeling is employed as a means of communication between an Alpine male and his girl. It is added, however, that this form of yodeling is not differentiated from that used for other purposes. Even though it is employed as means of communication between the two, it has many more general characteristics than would be found in a form which is only dictated by the sexual drive.

Even though all these observations would seem to render Jaeger's views rather improbable, it must further be considered that yodeling would have to include other important elements for the progression to song if it were to be its origin. However, this is not the case. Among the primitive stages of development there is no vocal music without words. But the exclusion of words is precisely the characteristic mark of yodeling.

It is mentioned in one of the replies that "the more lonely the inhabitants of Alpine regions are, the less artistic is their yodeling and the less does it approximate the vocal song." We also have to add that several of the emotions which we discovered as important empirical sources of music, such as the mystic-religious emotion, do not permit their expression through yodeling.

Notes to the Essay

1. This essay had been submitted by Simmel as his doctoral dissertation to the Philosophical Faculty of the Humboldt University of Berlin. But his examining committee, composed of Professors Zupitza (chairman), Zeller, and Helmholtz, refused to accept it as submitted. Instead, they granted the degree for the previously written distinguished study on Kant's monadology. While Zupitza would have been willing to accept this study on music, if it were first "cleared of the numerous misspellings and stylistic errors," Helmholtz was more skeptical. "Regardless of my other reservations, Simmel is entirely too confident in his conclusions. And the manner

in which he presented the faculty with this piece which is so full of misspellings and stylistic superficialities, which evidently was not proofread, in which sentences which are cited from foreign languages can hardly be deciphered, does not attest to a great deal of reliability. Insofar, however, as he has quite a few illustrious predecessors for what he evidently takes to be the method or lack of method of scientific study, he may let them serve as some kind of personal excuse. I, however, believe that we will be doing him a greater service if we do not encourage him further in this direction." [Michael Landmann, "Bausteine zur Biographie," in Kurt Gassen and Michael Landmann, *Buch des Dankes an Georg Simmel*, Berlin: Duncker and Humblot, 1958, p. 17.] As becomes evident from our text, Simmel must have published his study without paying heed to his professors, since footnotes and textual quotations reflect the shortcomings already criticized. Where it was possible to discern Simmel's likely source, fuller bibliographic information was supplied. We also compiled a bibliography of the works which Simmel might have used for his study (Appendix B). Hence, as chaotic as the documentation may still appear, it is already "improved" over Simmel's original.

2. *The Descent of Man*, 1874, p. 595. The identical thought already occurred to Leibnitz. He observes, however: "One must also consider that man could speak, that is, make himself understood by the sounds of the mouth without forming articulate sounds, if one were to use musical tones for this effect. But it would need more art to invent a language of tones instead of that of words formed and perfected by degrees, by persons living in the natural simplicity." [Leibnitz, Nouveaux Essais sur l'entendement humain, III, 1.]

3. *Über den Ausdruck der Gemütsbewegungen*, 1872, 88.

4. Cited by Steinthal from *Ausland*, 1867, No. 42.

5. The more the linguistic capacity increases, the more will automatic reflexes of this variety be drawn into the realm of language. This goes so far, if one is very strongly habituated to the use of language, that one will exclaim words even in situations which almost incapacitate us, and which in a natural state would produce only inarticulate shouts. When there is a sudden feeling of fear, we call out "Heaven!" or "Jesus!" and the like.

6. One might wish to compare here tonal modulations which are much more frequently employed for the significance of meaning in lower languages than in our own.

7. Lazarus, *Leben der Seele*, II, 136.

8. Humboldt, *Einleitung zur Kawisprache*, Paragraph 9.

9. Cicero, *De oratore*: "Accentuation is employed in learning indistinct melodies." And during the Middle Ages it was said: "The accent is the mother of music."

10. Mere noise can be produced from musically pure tones by, for example,

the simultaneous pressing of all the keys of a piano within several octaves. Compare Helmholtz, *Tonempfindungen*, 14.

11. Toole, *The Diversions of Purley*, 62.

12. Freycinet, *Voyage autour du Monde*, I, 153.

13. Hochstetter, *Neu-Seeland*, 509.

14. Martius, *Ethnographie Brasiliens*, I, 330.

15. Grey, II, 301 ff.

16. Compare Poeppig, *Reise in Chile*, I, 332.

17. As is already exemplified above, Brahmans say that music is given to them by Sarasvati, the goddess of speech. Plato considers all music without text worthless (*Politics*, II), as does Augustine (*Confessiones*, K. 50). Likewise, Herder (*Ideen zur Geschichte und Kritik der Poesie*, No. 33). Kant, however, includes only music without words among the "free beauties" (*Urteilskraft*, Paragraph 16).

18. When Lully used to compose his beautiful recitatives he would sometimes request the "Chamesse" to declaim to him the work, take the tones rapidly, and then reduce them to the rules of Art. (Batteux, *Les Beaux Arts*, 258).

19. Bodenstedt, *Gesammelte Schriften*, III, 121.

20. Cicero, *Pro Archia*, 19.

21. Musters, *Unter den Patagonern*, 185.

22. Appun, *Tropen*, II, 298.

23. Smith-Hamilton, *Natural History of the Human Species*, I, 156; Schweinfurth, *Quer durch Afrika*, I, 450. Compare, however, Soyaux, *Aus West-Afrika*, II, 176–179.

24. Bowdich, *Mission nach Ashanti*, p. 465.

25. Schlagintwelt, *Californien*, p. 338.

26. See Petermanns, *Mitteilungen*, 1856.

27. Graul, *Reise nach Ostindien*, II, 72.

28. Krieger, as cited by Bastian, *Mensch in der Geschichte*, II.

29. Aristides in *De Musica Libri*, I, 31, mentions that rhythm is observed through three senses, the visual sense by way of the dance, hearing by way of music, and tactile sense by pulse beats. Aristoxenus compares the various forms of rhythmic music with corresponding forms of pulse beats.

30. I know an elderly gentleman who continuously hummed to himself some little songs. He never produced them clearly and rhythmically, however,

as if he had been excited or angry. Excitement only produces an exaggeration of rhythmic faculties, which are always found in inhaling and exhaling.

31. Vischer, *Aesthetik*, Vol. 4, p. 980.

32. It is not at all precise. Whatever subjectively appears as the expression of moods, appears to the objective observer as their reflection. However, these reflections cannot be treated here in the narrow sense of the term.

33. It is not at all impossible that this rhythmic stamping is the origin of dance. Very likely, however, the dance is related to ordinary walking as vocal music is related to language. The very same forces which here led to rhythmic expression may have also done the same there.

34. Gerland-Waitz, VI, 78.

35. Brugsch, *Reiseberichte aus Aegypten*, 254.

36. Le Gobien, *Histoire des Isles Marianes*, 406. Adelbert von Chamisso, who travelled there one hundred years later, still does not find any form of instruments there. *Entdeckungoereise*, I, 133.

37. Salvado, *Memorie storiche dell' Australia*, 306.

38. Westphal, *Geschichte der alten Musik*, I, 95.

39. Schlagintweit, *Reisen in Indien*, II, 92.

40. Cited in Darwin, *The Descent of Man*, 1874, p. 593. Such bone flutes belonging to the earliest cultural period are also found in South America. Examples can be found in the South America section of the Ethnographic Museum, Copenhagen. In the Italian language, *ossa* is the translation of *pipe* (Boccaccio, *Decamerone*, III, 10). The human tibia is used in Tibet as a musical instrument (Turner, Gesandtschaftsreise nach Tibet, 349). In Angela, Hamilton heard a curious double clarinet which was formed of the leg bones of the eagle or vulture (Hamilton, Wanderung in Nord-Afrika, 213.)

41. Seeman, II, 67.

42. Delaborde, I, 157.

43. Andree, 197.

44. Hupel, *Topographische Nachrichten*, II, 133.

45. Gerland-Waitz, VI, 77.

46. Ibid., p. 604

47. Sartorius, "Zustand der Musik in Mexiko," *Caecilia*, VII.

48. Bossmann, *Reise nach Guinea*, 170.

49. Freycinet, I, 663.

50. Wilkes, *Exploring Expedition.*

51. In New Guinea even captured human skulls are filled with stones, hard kernels of food, and pumice stone, and used as rattles. Exhibits are in the Museum of Godeffroy as reported by Andree, *Enthographische Parallelen,* 140. Rattles were also found in very ancient German tombs. One exhibit is in the Sammlung der Deutschen Gessellschaft in Leipzig. Concerning others and the relevant literature, see Ploss, *Das Kind,* II, 219.

52. Schweinfurth, *The Heart of Africa,* II, 34, found the most monotonous music among *Niamniamier.* These people have even a highly developed music aptitude which is expressed by their invention of instruments with properly constructed resonance bodies.

53. Quaas, *Beschreibung von Sansibar.*

54. *Bibliothek der Unterhaltung und des Wissens,* 1877, Vol. 10.

55. Tylor, *Anahuac: or Mexico,* 207.

56. Compare, for example, Krapf, *Reisen in Ost-Afrika,* II, 116.

57. Euler, *Briefe der Physik,* German Edition, Vol. 8.

58. Helmholtz, *Die Thatsachen in der Wahrnehmung,* Appendix F.

59. How very early distortions of music's natural state occur is shown by a fragment of Democritus (*Philodemus de mus.* IV, in Vol. *Hercules* I, page 135, col. 36). This view has been maintained until Burney expressed his erroneous point of view in the 1789 Preface to his *History of Music:* "Music is an innocent luxury unnecessary indeed to our existence, but a great improvement and gratification of the sense of hearing."

60. Bowring, *Siam,* 150.

61. Andree, *Das Amurgebiet,* 197.

62. Werder, *Zu den esthnischen Liedern.*

63. *Judges,* 5.

64. *Samuel* I, 2.

65. *Essay* I, 158.

66. D'Urville, IV, 707.

67. *Scipio apud Macrobium,* II, 10.

68. Vambery, *Sizzen aus Mittelasien,* 78 ff.

69. Musters, *op. cit.,* 67.

70. Gatteron, *Queer durch Afrika,* I, 163.

71. Chamisso, *Entdeckungsreise,* III.

72. Brisson, *De Regno Persarum.*

73. Busch, *Wanderungen zwischen Hudson und Mississippi,* I, 266.

74. Grey, II, 313; Gerland-Waitz, VI, 747 and 775.

75. Rochow, *Reise nach Madagaskar,* Forster, tr., 1792, 24.

76. Pirschewalski, *Reisen in die Mongolei,* 58.

77. An example is to be found in Schneider, *System einer medizinischen Musik,* I, 74.

78. Magyar, *Reisen in Südafrika,* I, 314.

79. Sirach, 9, 3.

80. Polak, *Persien,* 389; *Buch des Kawus,* 732; Brugsch, *Reise nach Persien,* 389.

81. Sprüche, *Salomon,* 5, 3.

82. See examples in Ploss, *op. cit.*

83. Dobritzhofer, *Geschichte der Abigonen,* II, 170.

84. Salvado, 306.

85. Bowdich, 468.

86. Jones, XII.

87. Mertens, *Recueil des Actes,* 146.

88. Pechuel-Lösche, (in) *Zeitschrift für Ethnologie,* 10 (1).

89. Waitz, III, 231.

90. Freycinet, I, 663.

91. Reade, *The Martyrdom of Man,* p. 441, and *African Sketch Book,* Vol. II, p. 313, as cited in Darwin, *op. cit.,* p. 595.

92. Brugsch, *Reiseberichte aus Aegypten,* 254 .

93. Weitzmann, *Geschichte der Griechischen Musik,* 23.

94. Pontecoulant, *Phenomenes,* 130.

95. Pindar, *Scholiast,* 9, 1.

96. A similar observation was already recorded by Aristotle who observes in *Politics,* XIX, 5, that we prefer to listen to familiar rather than unfamiliar music. Goethe observes, in similar fashion: "In its truest essence, music requires much less novelty. To the contrary, the older it is the more will one be accustomed to it, and the more effective will music then be."

97. Whether there are physical factors, such as differences between the form of the larynx and acoustical properties of hearing among various races

and people, which might be responsible for the preferred performance of certain songs and the avoidance of others, is unfortunately still a mystery for anthropologists.

98. Without any involvement of mystic elements.

99. Dallas, *History of the Maroons*.

100. Bowdich, 404 and 464.

101. Jones, 28.

102. Jourdain, V, 304.

103. Waitz, I, 157.

104. *Ibid.*, VI, 85. It seems to me that the observation seems to refer to the melody. That specialized linguistic formulas are employed on such occasions would seem to be self-evident.

105. Jonas, *Schweden*, 217.

106. Christ, *Pflanzenleben in der Schweiz*, 310–11.

107. Compare Waitz, *op. cit.*, VI, 651 as quoted from Erskine, 291.

108. Volkmann, 2nd edition, I, Paragraph 68, especially Addendum I. Also compare Spinoza, *Ethics*, Pars. IV, Proposition VII.

109. Especially the one acknowledged by Plato.

110. During the Christian Middle Ages the calming effects of music were emphasized. See for example Thomas Aquinas in his *Declarations Concerning the Canticus Canticorum* and the example of the fresco in the Capella degli Spagnoli. It is possible that the reason was partly the ascetic characteristics of these times which turned all naturalistic events into their direct opposite.

111. Salvado, 306.

112. It is the natural equilibration for the energy demanded by work. Music's connection with energy-demanding activities can become so firm that, conversely, it may also call forth energy.

113. Freycinet, 665.

114. M. Fabii Quintilian, *Institutionis Oratoriae*, I, X, 16.

115. Waitz, II, 67.

116. Review of Villoteau, by Hammer in vol. 56, *Wiener Jahrbücher*, 1831.

117. See for example, Freycinet, *op. cit.*; I, Waitz, *op. cit.*, II; Pontécoulant; Durand, *Voyage au Senegal*, and others.

118. Humboldt, *Ansichten der Natur*, I, Anmerkung, 51.

119. Baker, *The Nile Tributaries of Abyssinia*, 203.

120. Steinthal, *Der Ursprung der Sprache,* 3rd ed., 306. In a general sense these observations are probably correct even though Steinthal later considered the complete text from which his quotation is taken as antiquated.

121. Fechner, *Psychophysik,* II, 293.

122. Compare also Kant, *Urteilskraft,* Paragraph 51, 3.

123. "It is quite difficult not to surmise that our harmonies are nothing but Gothic and barbarian inventions of which we might never have become aware if it had not been for the truer and more artistic beauties of more truly natural music." Rousseau, *Dictionnaire de musique,* article on "Harmonie."

124. This can be most clearly illustrated by references to musical techniques and theory.

125. We can always see how important composers follow in the footsteps of their precursors before they develop their own styles. Goethe says that all true art will have to begin with "the tradition."

126. Bodenstedt, *op. cit.,* II, 104.

127. Polak, 292

128. Ambros, *Geschichte der Musik,* II, Preface, XXII ff.

129. I believe I am entitled to think that relevant literature does not exist. The exception is a small, valueless report by von Sieber, "Das Jodeln der Bergbewohner," in *Echo,* No. 43, 1853. (For Simmel's questionnaire see Appendix A, following.)

130. There is a single contradictory fact which was reported to me. Genuine yodeling was observed once among the natives of Hasserode in the Hartz mountains. Since this is a single case it may have to be related to some accidental causes such as, perhaps, historical migrations of south German Alpine peoples to these regions.

Appendix A to the Essay

Questionnaire on Yodeling by Georg Simmel *

To the S. A. C.:

In the interest of anthropological research, which aims at assigning an appropriate place to the curious phenomenon of yodeling within the history of human forms of expression, I request answers to the following questions. Moreover, I request information concerning possible existing literature on this subject. I would also like to request that attention be paid

* Translated from *Jahrbuch des Schweizer Alpenclub,* 14:552–554, 1878–9.

to it, and that it be observed if the occasion should present itself. If from previous experience and recollections, it should already be possible to provide exact answers to these questions, I request that they be answered not with a simple "yes"—if the answer should be positive—but instead so as to provide as precise information as possible concerning the situation under which the observations occurred, as only then can a psychologically valuable conclusion be drawn, in particular with respect to questions numbered 5, 8, 11, 14, and 15. In addition, I request correspondence on all other observations concerning yodeling which are not anticipated in my subsequent questions; I would also greatly appreciate any transcriptions of yodelers in musical notation.

1. Between what ages do inhabitants of the mountains engage in yodeling?
2. Are there specifically different types of yodeling found in one and the same region?
3. Do different types of yodeling exist in different mountain areas, and how do they differ?
4. Are there any observations which indicate that perhaps the altitude of the places of residence is related to differences in yodeling, and if so, how?
5. What is the relationship between the spoken language and yodeling?
6. What are the surrounding circumstances under which yodeling is generally practiced?
7. In which cases is it employed for special, practical purposes of communication?
8. Can it be established that yodeling is a purely acoustical reflect of emotions, i.e., are there certain emotions for which the inhabitants of the mountain regions seek an expression through yodeling irrespective of whether they are being listened to or even of listening to themselves, comparable to one's crying and groaning in response to pain?
9. What kinds of emotions are these? Are they, for example, those of sexual excitement?
10. Can it be established that yodeling serves as a medium of communication between boys and girls, similar to some *Schnadehüpfeln,* even if not directly comparable to the purposes of the mating call among animals, though, nevertheless, a sign of mutual inclination and agreement? Or does it serve related purposes if only from one side?
11. How important for the exercise of yodeling are the factors of habituation, of its enjoyment and of the ambition to be able to yodel with greater perfection than the others? Also with respect to the opposite sex?
12. Do women also engage in yodeling? From which ages on? And, is it distinguished from the yodeling of men?
13. Is the enjoyment of playing with the echo, perhaps, a factor in the perfection of yodeling?
14. During the course of time is there a general decline in yodeling, perhaps, observable?

15. Has anything been observed in the regions outside of the Alps or in the flat terrain which is identical or only analogous to yodeling?

For relevant information, in complete subservience, asks

Georg Simmel

Berlin, W., Magdeburgerstrasse 31

Appendix B to the Essay

Bibliography of Titles Mentioned in the Text

Ambros, August Wilhelm, *Die Geschichte der Musik* (Breslau: Leuckart, 1882), 5 vols.

Andree, Richard, *Ethnographische Parallelen und Vergleiche* (Stuttgart: J. Maier, 1878),

Andree, Richard, *Das Amurgebiet und seine Bedeutung* (Leipzig: O. Spamer, 1867), 268 pp.

Appun, Karl Ferdinand, *Unter den Tropen* (Jena: H. Costenoble, 1871), 2 vols.

Ausland, *Berlin Universität, Seminar für orientalische Sprachen* (Berlin and Stuttgart: W. Speman, 1878).

Baker, Sir Samuel White, *Exploration of the Nile Tributaries of Abyssinia* (Hartford: D. D. Case and Company, 1864), 624 pp.

Bastian, Adolf, *Der Mensch in der Geschichte* (Leipzig: O. Wigand, 1860), 8 vols.

Batteux, Charles, *Les Beaux Arts Reduits a un Même Principe* (Paris: Durand, 1746), 291 pp.

Bodenstedt, Friedrich Martin von, *Gesammelte Schriften* (Berlin: K. Geheime Oberhofbuchhandlung, 1869), 12 vols.

Bowdich, Thomas Edward, *Mission nach Ashanti* (London: J. Murray, 1819), 512 pp.

Bowring, Sir John, *The Kingdom and People of Siam* (London: J. W. Parker and Son, 1851), 2 vols.

Brisson, Barnabe, *De regno Persarum principatu libri tres: Ex adversariis* (Paris: Apud Bartholomaeum Macaeum, 1606), 356 pp.

Brugsch, Heinrich Karl, *Reise der K. Preussischen Gesandtschaft nach Persien* (Leipzig: J. C. Hinrichs'sche Buchhandlung, 1863), 2 vols.

Brugsch, Heinrich Karl, *Reiseberichte aus Aegypten* (Leipzig: F. A. Brockhaus, 1855), 351 pp.

Burney, Charles, *A General History of Music* (London: Printed for the author, 1789), 4 vols.

Busch, Moritz, *Wanderungen zwischen Hudson und Mississippi, 1851–2* (Stuttgart und Tubingen: J. C. Cotta, 1854), 2 vols.

Cäcilia (Luxemburg: H. Oberhoffen, 1862).

Chamisso, Adelbert von, *Adelbert von Chamisso's Werke* (Leipzig: Weidmann, 1842), 6 vols.

Christ, Johann Ludwig, *Pflanzenleben in der Schweiz* (Leipzig: Vass, 1797).

Dallas, Robert Charles, *The History of the Maroons* (London: T. N. Longman and O. Rees, 1803), 2 vols.

Dallas, Robert Charles, *Geschichte der Maronenneger auf Jamaika* (Weimar: Im Verlag des F. S. priv. Landes-Industrie-Comptoirs, 1805), 356 pp.

Darwin, Charles, *The Descent of Man* (New York: Hearst and Company, 1874, revised and annotated edition).

Darwin, Charles, *Über den Ausdruck der Gemütsbewegungen* (Leipzig: F. A. Brockhaus, 1872).

Dobritchofer, Martin, *An Account of the Abipones* (London: J. Murray, 1822), 3 vols.

Dobritchofer, Martin, *Geschichte der Abiponer* (Wien: Joseph Edler von Kurzbeck, 1884), 3 vols.

Dumont D'Urville, Jules Sebastien Cesae, *Malerische Reise um die Welt* (Leipzig: Im Industrie-Comtoir [Baumgartner], 1837), 2 vols.

Durand, Jean Baptiste Leonard, "Voyage de Durand au Sénégal, fait dans les Années 1785 and 1786," *Collection de Voyages de L'Afrique* (Paris: Walcknaer, 1842), pp. 231–246.

Durand, Jean Baptiste Leonard, *A Voyage to Senegal* (London: Printed for R. Phillips, 1806), 181 pp.

Erskine, John Elphinstone, *Journal of a Cruise in the Pacific* (London: J. Murray, 1853), 488 pp.

Euler, Leonhard, *Letters Addressed to a German Princess on Natural Philosophy* (New York: Harper and Brothers, 1840), 2 vols.

Fechner, Gustav Theodor, *Elemente der Psychophysik* (Leipzig: Breitkopf und Härtel, 1857), 2 vols.

Freycinet, Louis Claure Desausles, *Voyage Autour du Monde* (Paris: Imprimerie Royale, 1824).

Graul, Karl, *Reise nach Ostindien über Palestina und Egypten von Juli 1849 bis April 1853* (Leipzig: Dorffling und Franke, 1856), 5 vols.

Grey, Sir George, *Journal of Two Expeditions of Discovery in Northwest and Western Australia* (London: T. and W. Boone, 1841), 2 vols.

Hamilton, James, *Wanderung in Nord-Afrika* (Frankfurt: A. M. Gaul and Bentelmann, 1856).

Helmholtz, Herman Ludwig Ferdinand von, *Tonempfindungen* (Braunschweig: F. Viewey und Sohn, 1863), 600 pp.

Helmholtz, Herman Ludwig Ferdinand von, *Die Thatsachen in der Wahrnehmung* (Berlin, 1879).

Helmholtz, Herman Ludwig Ferdinand von, *On the Sensations of Tone as a Physiological Basis for the Theory of Music* (London: Longmans, Green and Company, 1875), 824 pp.

Herder, Johann Gottfried von, *Ideen zur Philosophie der Geschichte der Menschheit* (Berlin: G. Hempel, 1879), 700 pp.

Herder, Johann Gottfried, *J. G. Herder's Sämmtliche Werke* (Stuttgart: und Tübingen: J. C. Cotta, 1830).

Hochstetter, Ferdinand von, *Neu-Seeland* (Stuttgart: Cotta, 1863), 555 pp.

Humboldt, Alexander Freiherr von, *Aspects of Nature in Different Lands and Different Climates* (London: Longmans, Brown, Green, and Longmans, 1849), 2 vols.

Humboldt, Alexander Freiherr von, *Ansichten der Natur, mit Wissenschaftliehen Erlauterungen* (Stuttgart and Tübingen: Cotta, 1849), 2 vols.

Humboldt, Wilhelm von, *Einleitung zur Kawisprache* (Berlin: Druckerei der Königlichen Akademi der Wissenschaften, 1839).

Humboldt, Wilhelm von, *Über die Kawisprache auf der Insel Java* (Berlin: Druckerei der Königlichen Akademie der Wissenschaften, 1839), 3 vols.

Hupel, August Wilhelm, *Der Nordischen Miscellaneen* (Riga: J. F. Hartkooch, 1791), 17 vols.

Hupel, August Wilhelm, *Neue Nordische Miscellaneen* (Riga: J. F. Hartkooch, 1789), 10 vols.

Jahrbuch des Schweizer Alpenclub (Berlin, 1865).

Jonas, Emil Jacob, *Schweden und Seine Entwicklung in Volkswirthschaftlicher und Geistiger Beziehung Wahrend des Letzten Jahrzehnts* (Berlin, 1878).

Jourdain, John, *The Journal of John Jourdain—1608–1617* (Cambridge: Printed for the Hakluyt Society, 1884), 394 pp.

Kant, Immanuel, *Immanuel Kant's Kritik der Urtheilskraft* (Berlin: L. Meimann, 1869), 382 pp.

Kant, Immanuel, *Kant's Critique of Judgement* (London and New York: Macmillan and Company, 1882), 429 pp.

Krapf, Kurt, *Reisen in Ost-Afrika* (Zurich, 1880).

Lartet, Louis Marie Hospice, *Poteries Primitives* (Paris: Revue Archeologique, 1866), 24 pp.

Lazarus, Moritz, *Leben der Secle* (Berlin: F. Dummler, 1882), 3 vols.

Le Gobien, Charles, *Histore des Isles Marianes* (Paris: N. Pepie, 1700), 433 pp.

Leibnitz, Gottfried W. von, *Nouveaux essais sur l'entendement humain* (Paris: Charpentier, 1847).

Martius, Karl Friedrich Phillip, *Belträge zur Ethnographie und Sprachenkunde Amerikas, zumal Brasiliens* (Leipzig: F. Fleischer, 1867), 2 vols.

Magyar, Laszio, *Reisen in Süd-Afrika in den Jahren 1849 bis 1857* (Pest und Leipzig: Lauffer and Stolp, 1859), 1 vol.

Mertens, August, *Recueil des Actes* (Bonn, 1864).

Musters, George Chatworth, *At Home with the Patagonians* (London: J. Murray, 1871), 322 pp.

Petermanns Mitteilungen (Stuttgart: J. Maier, 1856).

Philodemus, of Gadara, *Philodem von der Musik* (Berlin: Bel H. Frolich, 1806), 64 pp.

Ploss, Hermann Heinrich, *Das Kind in Brauch und Sitte der Völker* (Stuttgart: A. Auebach, 1867), 2 vols.

Peoppig, Edward, *Reise in Chile, Peru, und auf dem Amazonenstrome* (Leipzig, 1836), 2 vols.

Polak, Jakob Edward, *Persien* (Leipzig: F. A. Brockhaus, 1865), 2 vols.

Pontécoulant, Adolphe Le Doulcet, *Les Phénomènes de la Musique, ou influence du son sur les etres Animes* (Paris: Librairie internationale, 1868), 159 pp.

Rochow, *Reise nach Madagaskar* (Berlin: Mittler and Sohn, 1880).

Rousseau, Jean Jacques, *Dictionnaire de Musique* (Paris: Chez la Veuve Duchesne, 1768), 548 pp.

Rousseau, Jean Jacques, *A Complete Dictionary of Music* (London: J. Murray, 1779), 468 pp.

Salvado, Rudesindo, *Memoires Historique sur L'Australie* (Paris: A. Pringuet, 1854), 443 pp.

Schneider, Peter Joseph, *System einer medizinischen Musik* (Bonn: C. Georgi, 1835), 2 vols., 352 and 380 pp.

Schweinfurth, Georg August, *Quer Durch Afrika* (Stuttgart: S. Low, Martin, and Searle, 1873).

Schweinfurth, Georg August, *Im Herzen von Afrika* (Leipzig: F. A. Brockhaus, 1880), 578 pp.

Schlagintweit-Sakunlunski, Hermann Rudolf Alfred von, *Reisen in Indien und Hochasien* (Jena: M. Costenable, 1880), 4 vols.

Schlagintweit, Robert von, *Californien* (New York: E. Steiger, 1871), 380 pp.

Smith, Charles Hamilton, *The Natural History of the Human Species* (Edinburgh: W. H. Lizars, 1848), 464 pp.

Soyaux, Herman, *Aus West-Afrika* (Leipzig, 1879).

Spinoza, *Ethica* (Leipzig: E. Koschny, 1875), 429 pp.

Steinthal, Chajim, *Der Ursprung der Sprache im Zusammenhange mit den letzen Fragen alles Wissens* (Berlin: F. Dummler, 1888), 380 pp.

Tooke, John Horne, *The Diversions of Purley* (Philadelphia: A. M. Duane, 1806), 2 vols.

Turner, Samuel, *Gesandtschaftsreise an den Hof des Teshen Lama durch Bottan und einen Theil von Tibet* (Berlin und Hamburg, 1801).

Turner, Samuel, *An Account of a Visit to Tibet* (London: sold by G. and W. Nichol, 1806), 473 pp.

Tylor, Sir Edward Burnett, *Anahuac* (Mexico and the Mexicans) (London: Longmans, Green, Longmans, and Roberts, 1861), 344 pp.

Vambery, Armin, *Reise in Mittelasien von Teheran durch die Turkmanische* (Leipzig: F. A. Brockhaus, 1873), 348 pp.

Villoteau, Guillaume Andre, *Musique de L'Antique Egypte* (Bruxelles: Degreef-Laduron, 1830), 80 pp.

Vischer, Friedrich Theodor, *Aesthetik Oder Wissenschaft des Schönen* (Reuttlingen und Leipzig, 1854).

Waitz, Theodor, *Anthropologie der Naturvölker* (Leipzig: F. Fleischer, 1872), 6 vols.

Weimarisches Jahrbuch fur Deutsche Sprache, Literatur und Kunst, Weimar, Hannover, 1857.